AF378469

TRAMS & BUSES OF WEST YORKSHIRE

Above:
A tranquil summer's afternoon in Keighley's North Street, about 1930, with Corporation 'trackless cars' loading for each of the town's major services. Brush-bodied No 15 (WU 2585), waiting at the Ingrow stand, is a 1925 Straker-Squire 50-seater, and was to see less than seven years' service.
Walter Scott (Bradford) Ltd

TRAMS & BUSES OF
WEST YORKSHIRE

A. E. Jones

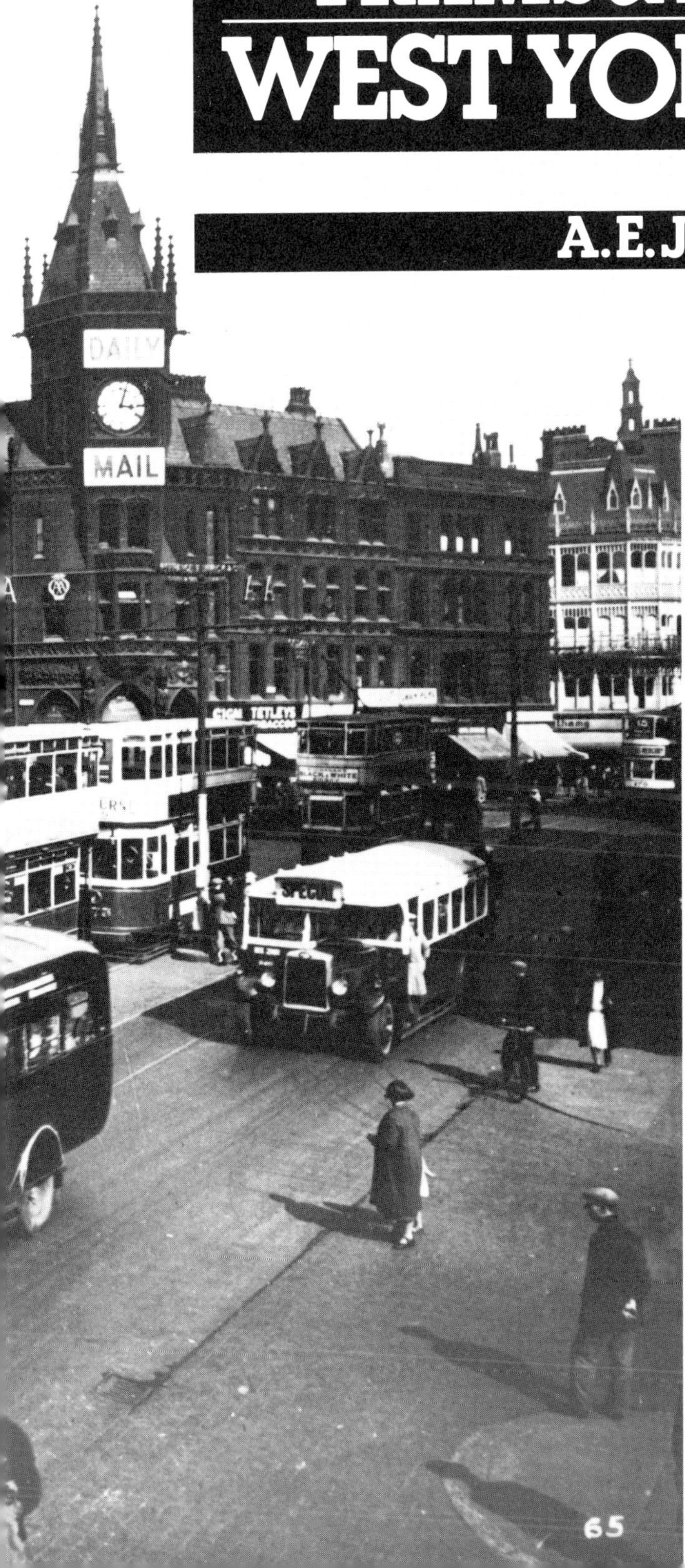

Contents

Previous page:
Slight blurring does not diminish the interest of a Northern General 1930 Short-bodied SOS (No 472, CN 4239), as it scurries through City Square, Leeds, heading for Liverpool. One of only a dozen SRR models built, all but two entered the NGT fleet when new in 1930: note the roof-mounted route indicator. It is hotly pursued by a West Yorkshire Road Car Roe-bodied Leyland Tiger TS2 of similar vintage (514, WX 2101), and three generations of Leeds trams fill in the background, together with a mid-1920s Corporation Dennis saloon. *Leeds City Libraries*

First published 1985

ISBN 0 7110 1470 1

Published by Ian Allan Ltd, Shepperton, Surrey; and printed by Ian Allan Printing Ltd at their works at Coombelands in Runnymede, England.

Introduction

In researching my first book, *Roads & Rails of West Yorkshire*, I unearthed a wealth of photographs, many of which I was unable to use in that volume. Space restrictions also enforced curtailment of the story at a time before the memory of any enthusiast much younger than 40 or so. The publisher has now kindly afforded an opportunity of remedying both situations to some degree, although the region has been so full of transport interest that, even now, less than justice can be done to the subject, and there still remain good views of interesting rolling-stock which have had to be excluded.

In *Roads & Rails*, the choice of photographs was governed by the text; balance across operators and the time-span was essential. In this album, other considerations can apply, and I have been more-influenced by subject-interest or pictorial merit than other factors. The other major difference within these pages is that topics take precedence over strict chronology.

I now also have chance to set the record straight on a few errors I unwittingly perpetrated. To the residents of Outlane (Huddersfield), my apologies for splitting the name of their district in two, and to Hanson enthusiasts for stating that the company was an ardent buyer of Albion chassis in prewar days. Such is the dearth of information on some sizeable Yorkshire fleets, and deadlines too short to check *every* detail, that I had to assume that some impressions I held some 35 years ago were valid, and it proves, if nothing else, that postwar Albion buses looked very old-fashioned! Remember, there were no area fleetbooks to give the correct version in those far-off days. Hanson's had in fact been a Leyland fleet until the mid-1930s, but a leavening of AECs from 1931 became the staple diet five years later. Albions did not appear on stock until 1941, and only 14 examples were purchased altogether, over an eight-year span; I must have seen them all in service together!

West Yorkshire Road Car's Tilling-Stevens B9As had straightforward mechanical transmission, and not petrol-electric drive, which had last featured in the TS6 deliveries of a year earlier (1926). The Holmfirth independent referred to in Chapter 9 was Walter Bower (*not* Blower), who was bought-out jointly by Huddersfield Corporation and Hanson's, and whilst there was a well-reported co-ordination scheme between the latter pair of operators in 1929, there was an equally-important one ten years later, in which a number of services were exchanged and territories redefined.

With regard to the Huddersfield-Bradford joint service, each of the three operators certainly used different route numbers for some years, but the two municipalities had standardised on '64' in the late-1930s, leaving only Hebble to persist in displaying '12' for another two decades. Confusion and loss of goodwill certainly arose in later days by the unilateral withdrawal of parcels facilities at different dates, intending consignors having to wait until a bus belonging to an operator still prepared to cater for this traffic came along! Hebble was certainly reported in the technical press of the day as ordering torque-convertor-transmission Leyland Titans in the mid-1930s, but this must have been journalistic licence, or perhaps wiser counsel prevailed in time to forestall despair!

I am indebted to Mr Geoff Lumb for the corrections on operators in the Huddersfield area, and would also like to thank Messrs D. Akrigg, L. J. Patch, D. Whiteley, and J. S. King, for further information on Hebble and Bradford Corporation. Once again, I would also express my appreciation to all those whose photographs were made available, and to the PSV Circle whose publications have provided much of the detail on vehicle acquisitions and disposals. The valuable assistance given by my original sources has also been carried forward into this book.

Right:
The only dependable vehicles of their day for Halifax's difficult terrain, in such treacherous weather, a Corporation 'Pullman' and an older balcony car await departure in Commercial Street.
B. Fielding

Below:
A Leeds Middleton Bogie car at Lingwell Road terminus, newly-resplendent in the early postwar livery of pale blue and cream.   *A. D. Packer*

Below right:
The primary subject of this 1934 view is of secondary importance to the Chevrolet LM-model 14-seater (WW 2103) standing in Bondgate, Otley. Seen here in service with local operator Fred Rathmell, who sold out to Ledgard in 1936, it had started life in 1927 with Sutcliffe's of Mytholmroyd.
Walter Scott (Bradford) Ltd

12
SWINEGATE
VIA MOOR ROAD
258

1
First Footing

The horse bus had first appeared in recognisable form on London's streets, in 1829, and came to the provinces at a fortuitous time as an urban specialisation of the stage coach, when the latter was declining rapidly in the face of the expanding railway system. Indeed, some of the earliest horse buses in West Yorkshire provided feeder services from stations on the newly-opened Manchester & Leeds Railway, to towns like Keighley, Bradford, Halifax, and Huddersfield, from 1840 onwards, until further railway expansion made them redundant.

It also became a means of purely local transport as the Industrial Revolution made its impact on the size of towns, and the first urban services appeared in Leeds and Wakefield in the same year. However, other towns in the region did not develop a sufficiently large middle-class sector who could afford to use them, quite so early, remained more compact to a later date, and were rather too hilly to encourage such speculation. The economics of horse bus operation were not conducive to cheap fares, three horses and two men being necessary for a vehicle with a maximum capacity of 27 passengers.

Carriers' carts would take the less-well-to-do passenger beyond the town limits, if packet boats on the canals and river navigations could not suffice, and later diversification into horse-drawn wagonettes and *chars-a-banc* came only as the bulk of the population rose above subsistence level, well after the factory system had become established.

However, by the 1880s the demand was there, and undertakings like John Marsh or Tillotson's of Halifax were providing local services to Salterhebble, Pellon, Warley, Rishworth, and up Calderdale, as well as 'Countryside Tours' to Blackstone Edge, Nont Sarah's, Denholme, and Cragg Vale. Both here and in Wakefield the lack of tramways led to more intensive coverage than elsewhere, but Bradford also had well-developed town services of buses and wagonettes

(if infrequent at times) along 14 lines of route, in this era; the last ran in April 1904, to West Bowling.

The advent of horse and steam tramways impacted on this form of transport, of course, but attention could often be turned to districts which could not justify the costs of rail-bound transport, particularly as the turnpikes disappeared and the new County Council and County Boroughs got into their stride, in the closing years of Queen Victoria's reign.

With the benefit of hindsight it is easy to criticise the tramway-building local authorities for selecting incompatible track gauges, which would later preclude through services between adjacent systems. However, it should be remembered that when such irrevocable decisions were taken, interurban journeys were the prerogative of the railways, the inexorable extension of urban areas towards each other had proceeded so far within the lifetime of those making the decisions that significant further expansion must have been considered as limited, and the need for mass travel to the next town must have seemed a remote possibility. Each large urban area, particularly in West Yorkshire with its added topographical constraints, was virtually a self-contained social and economic unit, with a very clearly-defined sphere of influence. Only the unfortunate instance of the Dewsbury & Ossett Tramway can truly be said to have been a short-sighted decision, and there the problem was parochial pride, and not technical factors.

One might also be tempted to criticise the reluctance to continue expansion of individual systems after the initial euphoria had died away (c1907), but a vast municipal debt had been amassed by that time, one of the recurrent slumps in economic activity was depressing investment, and the gadfly attentions of some local councillors had doubtless switched to other forms of traction. The basic error, almost universally, was to fail to make adequate provision for future repairs and renewals.

Above:
A wagonette with *chars-a-banc* **seating outside the Fox & Hounds Inn, Newmillerdam, in 1897. Such vehicles were usually the only form of interurban road transport before the advent of the electric tram and motorbus, as well as being popular for short-radius excursions, as in this case.**
Wakefield Art Gallery & Museums

Right:
A Wakefield City & District Omnibus Company's three-horse team thunders across the city's Chantry Bridge, in pre-tramway days.
Wakefield Art Gallery & Museums

Above:
Less flamboyant than its predecessors, Leeds Corporation's last horsebus is posed in Kirkstall Road Depot on retirement in 1911, having displaced the city's first motorbuses on a feeder service from the Lower Wortley tram terminus some five years earlier. *Leeds City Libraries*

Centre left:
Typical of conventional horse tramway rolling stock, this example trundled from Keighley to Utley and Ingrow for 15 years, having been built by Starbuck of Birkenhead in 1889. *I. Dewhirst*

Bottom left:
The August 1882 opening of the Leeds Road steam tramway in Bradford is recorded here, the scene portraying a Kitson horizontal-boilered engine hauling an Eades reversible trailer. The unusual semi-covered top deck protected at least some upstairs passengers from smoke and cinders. *Bradford Telegraph & Argus*

Top right:
A much more potent-looking Kitson locomotive of 1889 poses in Lockwood Road, Huddersfield. The massive passenger car was one of a pair built by G. F. Milnes two years earlier, and had originally been open-topped.
Kirklees Libraries & Arts

Centre right:
The initial 58 cars supplied to Halifax between 1898 and 1902 by Milnes of Birkenhead had Peckham trucks of only 5ft 6in wheelbase, and are represented here by No 45, on Gibbet Street about 1905. The conductor does not sport a ticket punch as fares were collected from every passenger on board at each successive fare stage, without receipt, until 1908.
Bernard Fielding Collection

Below:
Halifax 94 was from a batch of eight cars purchased from Brush in 1904 and was involved in the system's first fatal runaway accident on 1 July 1906, when it overturned on North Bridge. Rebuilt with a top-cover, it was used as a Forces recruiting car in 1914, and then gave a further 20 years service.
Alice Longstaff

Above:
A hive of commercial activity in Bridge Street, Bradford, in
Edwardian days. Car 87, a 1902 Brush product in original
open-top condition, reverses for a trip to Duckworth Lane,
whilst behind it stands a similar vehicle modified by the
addition of a Bailey top-cover.   *Walter Scott (Bradford) Ltd*

Below:
A Yorkshire (West Riding) Electric Tramways car (No 24) of
the initial Liverpool pattern with extended canopies, as
supplied by Dick, Kerr, of Preston in 1904, runs into
Pontefract on the isolated line from Normanton and
Castleford.   *Wakefield Art Gallery & Museums*

One of four extra-short 20-seater trams of the Yorkshire (Woollen District) system at Moorend terminus, Cleckheaton, in 1905, which had been built the preceding year by Brush of Loughborough. Twenty years later it was to be 'married' to another car of the same batch to produce an extra 33ft-long tram for the Ravensthorpe service, as shown below.   *Yorkshire Woollen District Transport Co*

2

'Let's Try One of Those!'

Largely because of the cramping legislation of the 1870 Tramways Act, electrification came rather late to most British systems, although three of West Yorkshire's major undertakings (Leeds, Bradford, and Halifax) were getting into their stride as the new century dawned, and Huddersfield was not far behind. The hilly terrain which most of them had to contend with ensured that short-wheelbase two-axle cars were the norm, seemingly a retrograde step after 20-years use of long eight-wheel trailers on many steam-tram services. Apart from an experimental pair in Leeds, only Huddersfield attempted to use bogie cars on an electric system before World War 1, and even they were retrucked as rigid four-wheelers early in their careers; the difficulties of applying effective brake-gear to bogie designs was the major stumbling block, as the traditional handbrake was insufficient to control cars on many routes. Single-deckers were to be seen only on the Yorkshire Woollen District system, in the early years, apart from the American-built trams of the pioneer Roundhay line in Leeds, which had opened in 1891, and two demi-cars in Halifax.

Given the intemperate climate, it was not surprising that attempts were soon being made to boost revenue by enclosing open top-decks, but fear of overturning-accidents meant that a wide variety of half-measures in this direction were attempted, particularly in Huddersfield, and the parsimony of company operators like Yorkshire Woollen resulted in many makeshift conversions. The first fully-enclosed car was not seen until an isolated example was put into service by Huddersfield in 1910, and another 13 years elapsed before any further examples entered service there, and also in Leeds.

As recorded before, the first motorbus was put into service in Bradford for a short period as early as 1900, but 1905 turned out to be the climactic year for this new form of transport, with successful independent operations instituted in the Keighley area, Leeds Corporation's less-than-happy experience with tramway feeder services, and the de Dietrich illustrated here, which was run by a private proprietor to connect Yeadon with the Leeds tramways, which had then reached Horsforth. The following year saw the institution of a steam-bus service in Harrogate, to Oatlands, Bilton, and New Park, followed shortly by a 'country route' to nearby Knaresborough. Lest this should be thought a questionable step, such vehicles were practicable machines by contemporary standards. In using paraffin fuel to produce high-pressure steam, they did not require a chimney to induce a draught, and avoided most of the problems associated with the transmissions of their petrol-driven rivals. A dozen were acquired by 1909, and ran for up to eight years. It has great relevance to this story, as the foundation of today's West Yorkshire Road Car Company.

The permanent introduction of motorbuses by Todmorden Corporation occurred in 1907, Keighley following suit a year later, but the main impetus then passed for a while to private operators who, often operating motor lorries during the week, used alternative bodies to convert them for excursion work at weekends.

The second wave of expansion by the major operators came after 1910, with some limited tramway extension and rolling-stock improvements, and a determined commitment to motorbuses for feeder services by the Woollen District Tramways, and Leeds Corporation (again), as well as their rapidly-growing use by independent operators, some of whom would later become famous names in the industry. The most radical development, however, was the coincidental introduction of 'trackless tram' (ie trolleybus) services by Leeds and Bradford in May 1911, and by Keighley two years later. The outbreak of war in August 1914 had a profound and permanent effect, imposing a very different set of problems and priorities.

Right:
Reputedly the first motorbus in Yeadon, this de Dietrich chain-driven wagonette attracted a crowd of youthful admirers, when it materialised outside the Council Offices one day in 1905.
Bradford Telegraph & Argus

Below:
The Huddersfield General Carrying Company was primarily engaged in road haulage of wool, but seized the opportunity of converting this Commer Car 4-ton lorry to a 32-seater for excursion work each weekend. Reputedly the first charabanc to go over Holme Moss, CX 978 was requisitioned by the War Department in 1914, and went to France with the 4th Div Ammunition Company.
G. P. H. Dyson

Left:
Straker-Squire chassis were commonplace on London's streets in the pioneering days, doubtless prompting the Huddersfield General Carrying Co to purchase this elegantly-bodied charabanc. CX 2176 was snapped on a chapel outing from Heckmondwike.
G. P. H. Dyson

Above left:
Leeds Corporation's second foray into motorbus operation, in 1913, was more successful than the first, the greater reliability of vehicles like this London-style Daimler 40hp doubtless being the paramount factor. *Leeds City Libraries*

Left:
The same marque was also used by Yorkshire (Woollen District) in single-deck form, for pioneer bus services around Cleckheaton and from Ravensthorpe to Bradley, in 1913. This CC-type became a lorry after withdrawal in 1921: note the roof luggage-rack.
Yorkshire Woollen District Transport Co

Above:
Progress in tramcar design was so rapid after 1900, that the West Riding system altered its initial order for 55 cars on Dick, Kerr, of Preston to including balcony top-covers on the final 25. Car 42, seen here in Wakefield's Bull Ring on the Ossett to Agbrigg service when new, remained quite up-to-date for some years after delivery in 1905, apart from lacking windscreens.
Commercial postcard/D. J. Kerr Collection

Right:
Yorkshire Woollen's No 27 had been open-topped when built by Brush in 1902 and was fitted with this balcony top-cover after 1908, to bring it up to contemporary standards. The unequal number of side windows on the two decks gives the game away.
Yorkshire Woollen District Transport Co

Right:
Similar reconstruction of this 1900 Leeds tram, but retaining the short end-canopies, soon gained its class the nickname 'Bathing Vans'. Car 85 is seen at Victoria Road terminus in 1914 just after alteration. Eight cars of this pattern were sold to the West Riding system after its Castleford depot fire in 1917. *Leeds City Libraries*

Below right:
A less ambitious attempt at modernisation is portrayed by one of Huddersfield's original series, built as a bogie open-topper by Milnes in 1900. Car 7 had soon received a four-wheel truck, and gained its top-cover by 1912. It is seen here after final alterations in 1930, which included canopy extension and windscreen fitment. *The late Dr Hugh Nicol*

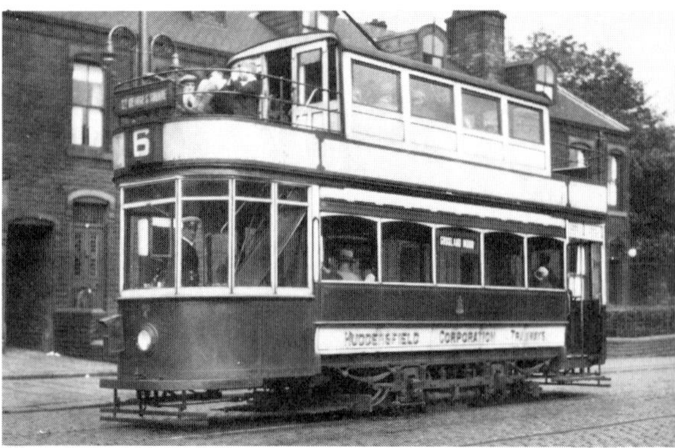

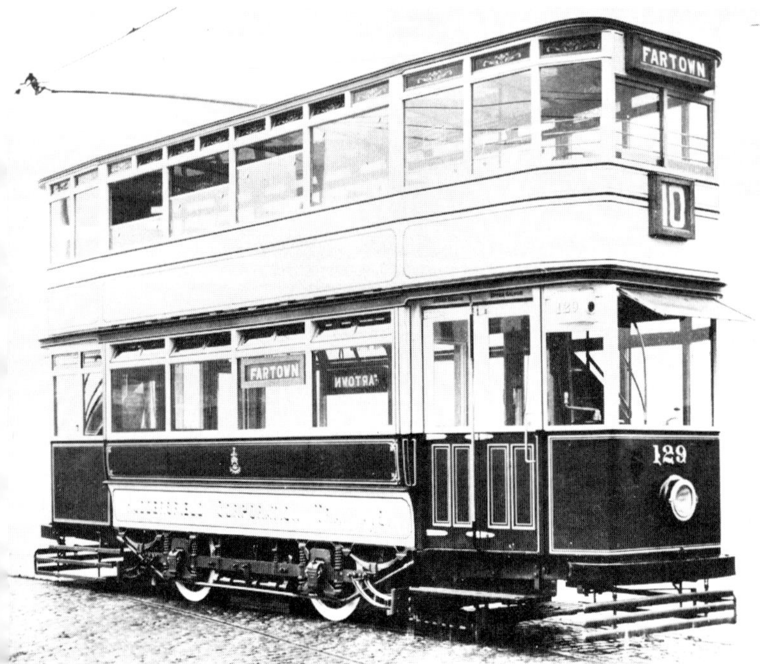

Left:
The ultimate goal of full enclosure was reached in Huddersfield with ten cars purchased in 1923 from English Electric. Although the advanced feature of platform doors had been specified since 1912, in deference to the exposed nature of some outer sections of route, previous deliveries had been built with balcony top-covers.
GEC Traction

3

Days of Wine and Roses

The tramway undertakings emerged from World War 1 in very poor physical shape, through deferred maintenance, overloading, loss of skilled staff, and revenues inadequate to offset even the sharp inflation in day-to-day expenditure which had occurred, and showed little sign of abatement. Industrial unrest, shortening of working hours, fuel shortages, economic depression, and legal restrictions on raising fares, did nothing to lighten the burden.

To this was added a flood of war-surplus chassis, a much greater interest in motorised transport, and a vast assortment of motor manufacturers trying to sell their excess wartime capacity on an over-supplied market. Any unemployed person with an ounce of enterprise was able to set up a bus service, provided a licence to ply for hire could be obtained from at least one of the districts to be served, and the general public naturally reacted with enthusiasm to the novelty, either because of its comparative speed in areas where tramways existed, or through availability of services not hitherto provided.

Having withdrawn all its initial motorbus services by 1915, Keighley Corporation recommenced operations in 1921, in the face of intense local competition, soon also using them to replace its highly-unreliable first-generation 'tracklesses'. Conversely, it invested in a fleet of more-conventional trolleybuses to displace the worn-out tramway system at the end of 1924. The first such wholesale abandonment in the region, this was followed within a year by the closure of the isolated Normanton-Castleford-Pontefract outpost of the West Riding company.

Halifax also had a brief dalliance with trolleybuses from 1921 to 1926, on a single route from Pellon to Wainstalls, but like Huddersfield and, above all, the West Riding Tramways, became an equally enthusiastic bus operator, whilst still doing its best to restore the tramway system to good shape. Yorkshire Woollen and Leeds Corporation expanded motorbus operation more cautiously, the latter also being in two minds about developing its trolleybus services, before deciding on retrenchment. Only Bradford clung solely to electric traction in the early-1920s, but was frustrated in its attempts to expand its trolleybus network.

The myriads of independent bus operators were able to run rings round the statutory undertakings, hampered only by the adamant refusal of the Leeds and Bradford Watch Committees from running services into the two cities, until both Ministry of Transport and local political pressure made such policies untenable. A number of famous names became firmly established in this era of cut-throat operation, like Ledgard, Bullock & Sons, Harrogate Road Car, Wallace Arnold, and Premier Transport, all with prewar antecedents, and newcomers to the scene like Hebble, Hanson, Blythe & Berwick, Feather's, North's Webster's, and many more.

The General Strike of 1926 gave most of them the chance they had been waiting for and consolidated the position of the stronger firms, who were increasingly absorbing their weaker brethren. Having demonstrated the demand for interurban services, there was no turning back the clock and, in retaliation, Leeds and Bradford could only hope to extend beyond their boundaries; in 1926 the latter was at last stung into motorbus operation, as a matter of self-preservation, but neither could get the powers they sought, for the time being. This period was also a watershed for vehicle design, as new low-loading chassis on pneumatic tyres at last began to be produced especially for bus use, and all-weather coaches began to displace open charabancs, heralding the start of long distance express services.

Such unbridled competition could not continue unabated, with the more-responsible operators disadvantaged by those who 'creamed' the best traffic, and disregarded public safety. By the end of the decade, legislation was at last enacted to help the railways combat the situation; it was also in preparation to bring order out of chaos on the road side of the industry. The latter, of course, unleashed a final flurry of warfare, as operators strove to position themselves to best advantage before the new traffic courts to be set up by the independent area traffic commissioners, under the 1930 Road Traffic Act.

Above:
Single-deckers began to assume a more conventional shape after World War 1. Keighley No 20 was one of the trio of Leyland G7s initially hired for reintroduction of motorbus services by the corporation in November 1921, to replace the Oakworth 'trackless cars'. *Keighley News*

Top left:
A neat little 18-seat Garford of F. P. Blakey, Otley, waits for time at White Cross, whilst a Leeds 'trackless car' glowers in the background. New in 1921, it passed to Blythe & Berwick three years later, but did not survive to the Road Car takeover of January 1928.   *Keighley News*

Centre left:
A semi-enclosed rear platform was the only concession to the rugged environment in which this early-1920s Karrier was operated by Baddeley Bros, on a tramway feeder service from Honley to Holme Bridge. The vehicle's radiator styling was very up-to-date, however.   *G. Mitchell Collection*

Below:
Leeds Corporation was also investing in buses with determination about this time, and these Dennis F-models delivered in 1926 with Strachan & Brown bodies were used in part to replace the Whitehall Road trolleybuses.   *Hestair Dennis Ltd*

Above:
A superb example of the traditional coachbuilder's art, this Todmorden 51-seat Leyland SG model was built in May 1924. Note the unusual position of the rear destination blind. *Leyland Vehicles Ltd*

Below:
West Riding Auto's 50-strong fleet of Bristol 2-tonners were very impressive machines for their day (1923/4), and gave up to nine years service. The crew of No 157 enjoy 'a breather' at the Airedale terminus.
Wakefield Art Gallery & Museums

Top left:
Pneumatic tyre development for heavyweight chassis was in its infancy when the Leyland SG-range was superseded by the Lion series, and this late example supplied to Todmorden in October 1925 must have been one of very few so fitted. Note the front entrance with folding step. *Leyland Vehicles Ltd*

Centre left:
Boroughbridge is a little beyond our territory, but this 1930 view well portrays the variety of rolling-stock to be seen then, even in the larger companies. The two buses on the right are unidentifiable, but that on the left (616, UM 8956) is a 1927 Dennis 30-cwt 19-seater acquired by the Road Car from Chapman's of Grassington in April 1930. *Walter Scott (Bradford) Ltd*

Below:
Following hard on the heels of Bradford's cumbersome AEC 413s, a batch of snazzy Leyland PLSC1 Lions arrived in the autumn of 1926. Their performance effectively countered Blythe & Berwick's competition, whilst their reversed livery gave a distinct lift to the city scene. *Leyland Vehicles Ltd*

Top right:
J. Bullock & Sons of Featherstone doubled the size of its fleet in 1924, and six Lancias with practical-looking 20-seat bodies by Bell of Finningley were amongst eight types of chassis purchased that year. The livery was red, with white roof. *Clark Photography/Courtesy Pontefract Museum*

Centre right:
West Yorkshire Road Car was avidly acquiring competitors in the late-1920s, and this PM28 model Albion (136, UM 7584) was absorbed in 1928 from J. Cole & Sons of Leeds. It had been delivered two years earlier, being fitted with a Strachan & Brown 32-seat body. *West Yorkshire Information Service*

Below:
Whilst the majority of Leyland Lions built were bodied by the chassis builders, B&S also patronised Clark of Scunthorpe, its design giving this 1928 32-seater PLSC3 model (86, WW 6771) a slightly more modern appearance. *Clark Photography/ Courtesy Pontefract Museum*

Top left:
The Bell bodies on the Lancias were good enough for further service and two were modified by the operator to fit on new Albion LC24 chassis in 1928; this is No 40 (WW 7378), which became a lorry for seven years, after withdrawal in 1932. *South Yorkshire Road Transport Ltd*

Centre left:
Squeezing its way through a tight spot in Braithwaite or Haworth is an ex-Keighley Brothers 1927 Leyland PLC1 Lioness which had been taken over by WYRC in June 1928. No 187 (CW 7162) has just been fitted with the framework for a standard 'bible' indicator, although the destination blind remains in place. *Leyland Vehicles Ltd*

Below:
Six-wheelers enjoyed a brief vogue at the end of the decade. The tramcar-style livery on Leeds 63 (UM 8083), an impressive 1928 Guy FCX with Roe 38-seat body, highlighted the obsolescent styling however, and it was a poor investment, giving only four year's service.
Leyland Vehicles Ltd

Above:
Much more in tune with the times were the Halifax Karrier WL6 six-wheelers. They also had short lives, however, due to shortcomings in mechanical design, although 46 (CP 6928) of 1929 somehow remained on active strength to 1934, when it was traded-in to AEC for a new double-deck Regent.
G. Mitchell Collection

Centre right:
Dennis Bros capitalised on its successful E-type by offering an optional six-cylinder engine in 1929. Leeds seized the opportunity of acquiring the resultant ES-model, alongside three other makes of chassis that year. The overall styling, including Edinburgh pattern cutaway rear-entrance on the 27-seat Roe body, gave No 87 a dated appearance, but the class survived until 1938.
Leyland Vehicles Ltd/Courtesy G. Lumb

Bottom right:
A different kettle of fish was this South Yorkshire Reo, its American origin betrayed by Trilex wheels. With a peculiar domed roof surmounting what looked more like a convertible open-topper, this potent machine entered the fleet in August 1929, and left the scene exactly four years later.
Clark Photography/Courtesy Pontefract Museum

4

A Time for Change

By the early 1920s, tramways were still using 30% of the electricity generated, in towns like Halifax, and although rolling-stock and track on many systems were in dire need of reconstruction, the capital debt was far from being paid off. Such were the conventions of municipal accounting, that tramway abandonment could not then be contemplated nor, indeed, was the motorbus a practicable alternative in crowd-clearing ability. Reasons such as these sustained interest in the primitive trolleybuses of the time, for secondary services with steady all-day traffic and minimal rush-hour peaking.

Exceptionally, Leeds had cleared its initial tramway debt by 1925, and embarked on replacing a fair proportion of its obsolete fleet, also improving track layouts. Elsewhere improvisation was the order of the day, although a limited number of new cars did appear on the other municipal systems, which in Huddersfield were totally-enclosed, whereas Bradford and Halifax had to be content with balcony designs. The latter pair did experiment with single-deckers in the mid-1920s, Halifax building three of conventional outline with detail variations, whilst Bradford's essay was a very unusual centre-entrance bogie-car which had coupled wheels, cardan-shaft drive, and air-operated doors, as well as a very high turn of speed. Perseverance would have sorted out the inevitable teething-troubles, primarily an inability to negotiate the sharper curves, but costs were too high for further examples to be sanctioned, in a period of economic stringency; although it remained popular with staff and passengers alike, it was an embarrassment in isolation, being ignominiously withdrawn within four years, in 1931.

When the new generation of motorbuses began to appear from 1925 onwards, the early trolleybuses were shown to disadvantage; other distractions apart, the nature of Leeds Corporation's operations led to their disappearance from that fleet within three years. In Bradford, on the other hand, they had been deployed to greater advantage, on services better-integrated with the tramways, headed by a general manager (R. H. Wilkinson) who was determined to progressively improve design to the point where they had become electric buses by 1927, rather than trackless trams. Hopes that they might totally replace the trams had been dashed by the Town Council, but within the next six years they were demonstrably superior to their petrol-driven contemporaries, apart from their reliance on an overhead power supply. The revenue which they contributed to the municipal electricity department and their eminent suitability for the city's many steep gradients made them the primary choice for tramway replacement thereafter. However, the conversion programme was long drawn-out by the incidence of car and track renewals in earlier years, given a policy of retaining such assets until the associated loan-capital had been fully-amortised; it was also inhibited by the difficulties of getting trolleybus powers over tram services which went beyond the city boundaries, not to mention the special problems of the post-1945 era.

In Huddersfield, the need for track and road reconstruction on the Almondbury route was the reason for the initial 1933 trolleybus experiment, but the arrival of a new manager from the very trolleybus-minded Nottingham undertaking at that crucial time ensured the implementation of a full conversion scheme, in spite of the recent acquisition of some thoroughly-modern new trams. Halifax was too deeply into debt with its existing system to contemplate further capital expenditure on fixed installations, as well as having a more geographically-restrictive Joint Committee scheme with the railways. The Woollen District's leases expired and would have dictated heavy outlays on new cars had they been renewed, at a time when the motorbus had fully matured, and the West Riding company had experienced 10 years of almost runaway success with its buses, as their system reached the end of its tether!

Above:

A Ministry of Transport edict apparently prevented Bradford from fully enclosing its tramcars, because of the narrow gauge and the many steep gradients. Car 74, built by BCT in 1924, therefore represented the final stage of development, and is seen in Forster Square on the Baildon Bridge service, when relatively new. *C. H. Wood (Bradford) Ltd*

Left:

The only concession to modernity on this Milnes-built Halifax car of 1900-vintage was the angular platform vestibuling fitted about 1926, and its retention in service for a further eight years did nothing to popularise the system. It ended its days in 1940 as a Home Guard post on Albert Promenade, below Savile Park. *H. B. Priestley*

Below:

Drawing on previous experience at Wigan, Ben Hall designed a trio of single-deck cars in 1924/5, primarily for the Queensbury route on which high winds were a source of concern for double-deckers. Equipped for passenger-flow with rear entrance and front exit on each side, No 105 became a caravan on Flamboro' Head after sale in 1935.
G. Mitchell Collection

Top left:
There was not much to choose between Leeds Pivotals and balcony cars in standard of ride, but the decrepitude of the latter was a matter of departmental concern by the mid-1930s. No 296 of 1913 vintage, with route number indicators added, waits to turn into Lower Briggate from Duncan Street on a rush-hour extra duty to Churwell Dye Works, in this mid-1930s view *A. K. Terry*

Centre left:
The Junction Inn, Moldgreen, is the 1920s setting for Huddersfield 92, a 1913 specimen from the United Electric Car Works, Preston, which had arrived in time for the Elland and West Vale extension and lasted until 1939. *Kirklees Libraries & Arts*

Below:
Halifax was also restricted to balcony designs, but the final trams built by the Corporation and English Electric between 1928-31 were much faster and more comfortable than their predecessors. No 121 of 1931, equipped with roller bearings, and upholstered seats, is seen in sheep country at Causewayfoot, at the end of its seven-year life.
H. B. Priestley

Above:
Leeds turned a new leaf with the practical Horsfield cars of 1930/1, although the chance to make a clean break from traditional styling was not seized. The first of the production series built by Brush, No 155 ran until closure of the system in 1959.
Leeds City Transport/Courtesy R. Marshall

Below:
In contrast to Leeds, Huddersfield had the courage of its convictions, and the English Electric cars of 1931/2 were thoroughly up-to-date when delivered. Car 137 was the first of eight, all later running in Sunderland from 1938 to 1954. *GEC Traction*

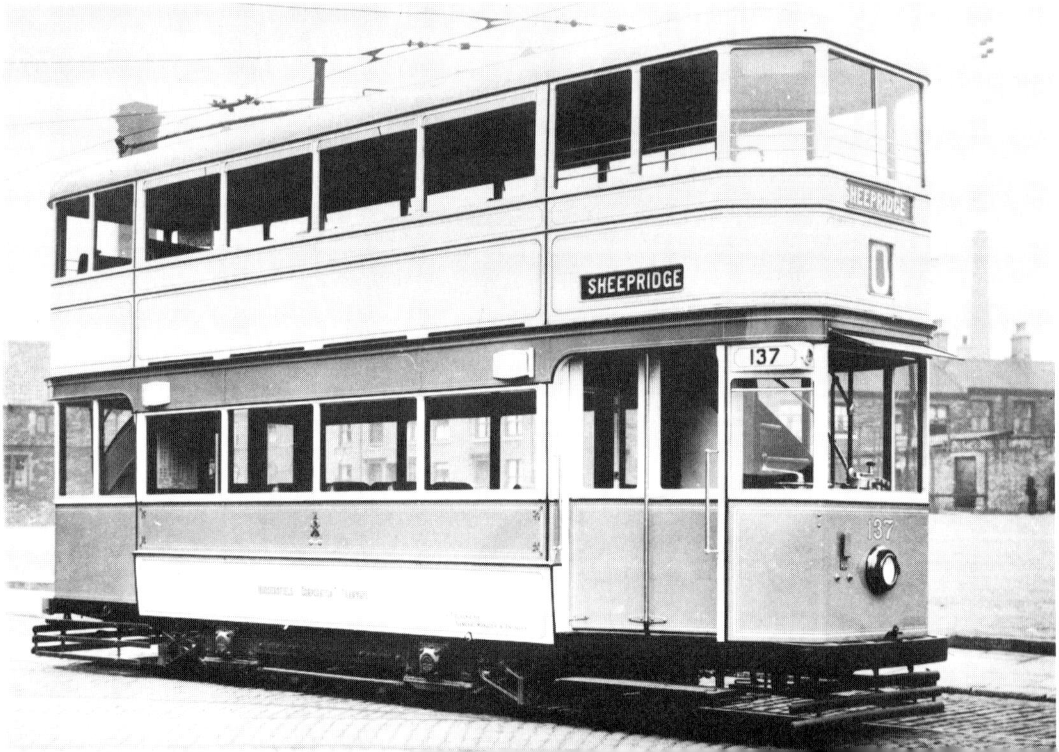

Bradford Telegraph & Argus

Left:
On the other hand, two of the initial
Leeds vehicles were rebodied as
passenger vehicles after the Great
War, to the 1915 (Guiseley section)
style, and one of these (503, U 8405)
was equipped with front-wheel
drive as a precursor to the ugly
double-decker illustrated in *Roads &
Rails of West Yorkshire*.
Keighley News

Left:
One of Keighley's
second-generation Straker-Squires
with Brush 50-seat bodywork built
in 1924, No 8 (WT 7104) remained in
service until closure of the system in
August 1932.   *I. Dewhirst*

Above:
Enigmatically numbered '522' in this builder's photograph, KU 1904 served the Bradford system as No 529, being one of three Associated Daimlers acquired in 1926. The Strachan 37-seat body looks more like a mobile waiting room than a bus, but it ran until 1937! Note the tramway-style lifeguard.
Bradford Corporation/Courtesy R. Marshall

Centre right:
A vast improvement was made with the styling of Bradford's 17 English Electric-bodied Leyland Lions delivered only two years later, and their demise was brought about by closure of the Oakenshaw service in the dark days of 1940.
GEC Traction

Bottom right:
The 25 double-deckers which arrived in 1929-31 proved to be the only six-wheelers purchased by Bradford (excepting the 'Chinese Six' of 1922), not being popular with drivers who often had to stand up to pull the steering wheel round! No 595 (KW 9464) was from the slightly less-angular second batch, all having English Electric 56-seat bodies; it was sold to Newcastle-upon-Tyne in 1942.
GEC Traction

Top left:
A further stage in modernisation is represented by Huddersfield 8 (VH 6751), a Brush-bodied Karrier E6 of the first production batch, for the Waterloo/Lindley/Outlane conversions of 1934. The illuminated direction arrows on the front dash were an experimental fitment. *R. Marshall Collection*

Centre left:
Bradford's AEC Q-type trolleybus was purchased late in 1934 after a seven-month demonstration period, and became No 633 (KY 6210). The doorless front entrance must have caused crews and passengers some consternation in wintry weather, and its single rear wheels made braking hazardous on sett-paved streets.
GEC Traction/Courtesy R. Marshall

Below:
Meanwhile, 36 conventional AEC 661T models were being equipped at Preston for the Thornton, Lidget Green, and Duckworth Lane conversions, marking the undertaking's permanent reversion to two-axle chassis. Durable machines, all were rebodied in 1944-49 and gave up to 28 years service: 597 and 609 are seen in Thornton Road when new.
Motor Transport

Right:
Only the simplified livery of the trolleybus and its 400-series fleet number prove this to be a postwar view of New Street, Huddersfield, as the cars and other detail are compatible with the late-1937 delivery date of this Park Royal-bodied Karrier E6, which was sold in 1950. *R. Marshall*

Above:
The AEC/English Electric formula was Bradford's primary choice again, in 1938/9, for the Wakefield Road and Manningham Lane conversions. In an early postwar view, No 669 rumbles over the bumpy stone setts in Forster Square, still looking very sound structurally, despite its faded and patched paintwork. *R. Marshall*

Left:
The Weymann bodies on the 16 contemporary Karrier E4s had a greater rake at the front, yet looked more severe, and the chassis were heavy on steering and more harshly sprung. Whilst most of them were rebodied in the 1950s together with the AECs, they therefore had shorter lives. *R. Marshall*

5

Municipal Musings

By 1930, motorbuses had assumed the general shape they would retain for another 20 to 30 years, although there were plenty of ungainly veterans in traffic then, and the final stages of refinement were still producing some unlikely variations. The major difference lay in the constitution of fleets, double-deckers being very much in the minority, partly because trams were catering for the heavier traffic flows, but also due to what is now a conventional height of vehicle having then been a very recent development.

Todmorden, Keighley, and Bradford, were then Leyland devotees, the former exclusively so, the latter also fielding ageing AEC and Bristol saloons, whilst Halifax and Huddersfield were embarking on an AEC buying-spree, after near-exclusivity on Karriers. Halifax had just had a strange dabble with demonstrators, its 1929 trio of Dennis, Karrier, and Leyland saloons, failing to clarify the undertaking's thoughts. However, the arrival of an open-staircase AEC double-decker concentrated minds to the extent that no other make of chassis was bought new until 1947, save for a pair of Leyland Cubs in 1939; these spent the war years in London on hire to the LNER, and were sold on returning, to Ripponden & District.

Secondhand acquisitions kept the Halifax engineers very busy, though, with the absorption of Albions, Commers, Gotfredsons, more AECs and Karriers, Leylands, and a Gilford! The Leylands included two of Hebble's initial SG models of 1925, plus some slightly-newer PLSC Lions from the LMS Railway; six out of 13 ex-Hebble buses allocated to the new Joint Committee were in such poor condition that substitute Leylands and Thornycrofts had to be hired from the LMSR and LNER.

In Leeds a consistent purchasing policy had been noticeable by its absence since 1927, and did not emerge until 1934 when AECs became the primary choice, with a make-weight of Leylands. Previously, various models of Crossleys, Dennises, Guys, Leylands, and even a Halley, had served the city to greater or less purpose.

All these undertakings were prepared to try the unconventional, excepting Todmorden, which liked what it had and stuck to it. Leeds fitted a Gardner diesel engine to a Crossley double-decker as early as 1930, and carried out comparative trials with AEC, Guy and Leyland chassis in 1933/4, subsequently standardising on oil engines. Halifax also made this change at the same time (1934), and Bradford a year later, where AECs became standard for a couple of years before a switch to Gardner-engined Daimlers. Gardner engines also became the Huddersfield preference from 1937, but were exceptionally specified in AEC chassis, after standard Southall-built diesels had been bought for two years.

Halifax's eccentricity was a surprise move in the opposite direction just before the outbreak of war, the general manager having supercharged petrol engines fitted to five 1939 Regents, thus explaining the illustration of a gas-producer trailer behind one of that year's deliveries in *Roads & Rails of West Yorkshire*.

Given the amount of tramway conversion and general traffic growth which occurred in the 1930s, it is not surprising that single-deckers were in the minority by 1940. Bradford did not acquire any more until the mid-1950s, whilst Leeds only bought a token pair of half-cab Leyland Tigers in 1948 before needing to withdraw its prewar Tigers in 1954. The 'standee' craze then being in full swing, the replacements were very unpopular in having only 34 seats, to allow a further 24 standing passengers to be crammed in. This feature, together with their very high floor level, made them totally unsuited to the extremely hilly cross-suburban routes on which they were normally employed.

Both Halifax and Huddersfield had greater need for single-deckers, with more thinly-populated territory to cover, and therefore had to seriously invest in half-cabs immediately after the war. Whilst Halifax remained faithful to AEC, Huddersfield had to buy Daimlers to maintain standardisation on Gardner engines, and then switch to Guy Motors for its earliest underfloor-engined models, from 1951 onwards.

Above:
Leeds switched totally to double-deck buying for its 1930 programme, the Crossleys being the shortest-lived of the three competitive makes bought in that year. No 104 (UA 5854) was a 48-seater Condor with Leyland-inspired bodywork, which gave five years service before sale to Cardiff Corporation.
Leyland Vehicles Ltd/Courtesy G. Lumb

Below:
Experiments were still being made with alternative petrol-engined chassis in 1932, but the 52-seater Roe body on Leeds 125, a Dennis Lance II, represented a great leap forward, and the style would survive in the city's fleet for 25 years. Stored after withdrawal in 1938, it became an ARP vehicle in World War 2.
Leyland Vehicles Ltd/Courtesy G. Lumb

Left:
Bradford stood out against local trends, and switched allegiance from AEC to Daimler in the mid-1930s. A Weymann-bodied COG6 model of 1936, 435 (AKW 435) operates a rush-hour special at the end of its days, showing 'Duplicate Bus' in lieu of a route number.
R. Marshall

Left:
Huddersfield 125 was an AEC Regent demonstrator which accordingly had Middlesex registration CMC 269. Built early in 1935, it was also Park Royal's first metal-framed highbridge body.
Park Royal Vehicles Ltd/Courtesy R. Marshall

Left:
Leeds 76 (FNW 46) of 1937 was the sole Weymann-bodied 'decker in the prewar fleet, apart from the 'streamliner' displayed at the 1935 Commercial Motor Show. It survived for 19 years, although relegated to training duties from 1949. One of the many contemporary Roe-bodied Regents ticks over in the background.
Leeds City Libraries

Above:
By the time this Huddersfield bus was delivered in June 1938, Gardner GLW engines were being specified, requiring an even longer bonnet than their Halifax contemporaries. The Park Royal bodywork order for this batch of only six vehicles was equally split between composite and metal-framed construction. No 140 was one of the latter, and is seen in the simplified postwar livery. *R. Marshall Collection*

Right:
The characteristic details of prewar Roe bodywork are highlighted in a latter-day view of a 1939 Halifax Corporation AEC Regent, parked in Cow Green. The projecting radiator was necessary because of standardisation on 8.8-litre engines to cope with the hilly terrain.
R. Marshall

Above:
'Halifax Corporation & Railway Services' says the emblem on the side, but this 1930 Leyland Tiger TS1 (151, WX 3260) had been a Ripponden & District bus until August 1934. It obviously did not strike a chord in the manager's heart, being sold off for better use elsewhere by the end of 1935, spending its declining years in Cambridgeshire.
Ripponden & District Motors Ltd

Left:
Single-deckers predominated in Bradford's fleet until the mid-1930s but thereafter the situation rapidly changed to the point where, for 15 years or so, only a handsome pair of Weymann-bodied 1936 AEC Regals were left, for which there were no regular services to operate.   *J. Copland*

Above:
Predictably, Leeds specified Roe bodies for its Leyland Tiger TS8s of 1938. Of BET Federation design, they became the backbone of the city's single-deck operations until replaced by underfloor-engined buses in 1954/5. Numbering of the city's bus fleet was somewhat erratic, and these saloons were allocated the sequence 19 to 26.
C. H. Roe/Courtesy R. Marshall

Above:
Huddersfield Joint Committee practice was to allocate alternate vehicles to corporation or railway stock, and so the legal lettering on No 65 (BVH 165), an AEC 0662 Regal of 1939, indicated LMS ownership. Gardner engine and Park Royal bodywork were again specified, as for double-deckers at that time.   *R. Marshall*

Below:
AECs continued in favour for double-deck work after 1945, but Huddersfield switched to Willowbrook-bodied Daimlers for saloon replacement. As Gardner engines were a standard fitment the change was not too extreme, and had probably been dictated by supply problems: No 90 was amongst two dozen built between 1948 and 1950, soon becoming obsolescent in the underfloor-engine era.
R. Marshall

Right:
Echoing the indecision of 25 years earlier, Leeds specified AEC, Guy, and Leyland chassis for the eight buses needed in 1954/5 to replace the prewar Tigers. All were fitted with 'standee' centre-entrance bodies by Roe, whose front-end styling suggested an unsolved problem on an otherwise pleasing design. Snapped here on a 'no-passport trip' to Lancashire, Leyland Tiger Cub 29 catches breath in Rochdale.   *J. B. Parkin*

6

Make Do and Mend

The most obvious impact the outbreak of war had in 1939 on public transport was the immediate implementation of the 'blackout' regulations. They reduced both internal and external lighting to a fraction of their former intensity, required white edging to be painted on the extremities of vehicles, roofs to be painted in dark colours, and anti-blast netting to be applied to all windows except for cabs and platforms. Destination indicator lights were usually dimmed by use of lower-wattage or blue bulbs, and crossings and section-breakers in tram and trolleybus overhead had to be shielded, to hide the arcing which occurred when current collectors passed under them.

Motor fuel allocations were progressively reduced, and vehicles could no longer be scrapped without special authority. In conjunction, these factors resulted in balcony trams reappearing in all-day service on the Leeds system, and the reconversion of the Undercliffe and part of the Shelf routes in Bradford, from motorbuses to trams. Both undertakings had to suspend their previous tram-replacement schemes, namely the elimination of the remaining single-line and loop routes in Leeds to Lower Wortley, Harehills Road, and Cardigan Road North, and the demise of the Wyke, Wibsey, and Queensbury lines in Bradford. The poor condition of the overhead in Cleckheaton Road did enforce the withdrawal of the Oakenshaw trolleybuses in 1940, however, and trams could no longer safely negotiate the tracks to Stanningley and Wyke after 1942 and 1944, respectively. Only the hiring of aged AEC Regents from London enabled service to be maintained on the former, and the arrival of utility buses make the latter possible.

Halifax had 'burnt its boats' by completing tramway conversion in February 1939, and relied solely on motorbuses, but had Huddersfield's trolleybus scheme started only a year later, it is likely that the last of its trams would have survived the war. As it happened, all the new trolleybuses had been delivered before PSV manufacture was suspended, and the last service, to West Vale, was converted only months behind schedule, in May 1940. Surprisingly, none of the remaining cars were sold for use elsewhere, their uncommon track-gauge of 4ft 7¾in scarcely being the engineering problem posed by the arrival of Hull cars in Leeds, or Bradford's in Sheffield, which occurred in 1942.

Long-distance travel was actively discouraged (coach services had been withdrawn, of course), and 'holidays at home' were official policy, throwing even more strain on local transport, to the extent that motorbus tours of the city were instituted in Bradford on summer weekends. The few remaining single-deck trolleys augmented services on Bolton Road, and at least one 1929 Leyland Lion bus emerged from four years' semi-retirement, whilst the few open-staircase Titans which had not been converted to Gardner diesel engines betrayed their presence on works services by crackling exhausts and clouds of blue petrol fumes.

Although new rolling-stock could not be obtained until the limited programme of utility bus-building was sanctioned, the local scene was enlivened by livery variations as substitute colours were resorted to, shades of grey or khaki becoming the most common. Strange vehicles also popped-up unexpectedly, London AECs appearing with West Yorks Road Car as well as Bradford, the former also operating East Kent and Halifax buses for a while; Leeds was briefly visited by Blackpool single-deckers, and Bradford for two years by Southend trolleys. On the other hand, a commendable percentage of the region's buses went to London's assistance in 1940-41, later helping in blitzed provincial cities such as Coventry, Hull, and Sheffield, as well as in other regions where extra vehicles were needed, like Deeside or Ulster.

An unexpected outcome of the blackout regulations led to Huddersfield acquiring its first-ever lowbridge double-deckers. A batch of utility Daimlers had to take over the Holme Valley services because normal-height buses were having too many confrontations with other traffic, when using the centre of the road to get under the railway arch in Lockwood; they were also useful in double-decking the Kirkheaton service.

Some of the company operators received significant benefit from the utility scheme, generally introduced from 1942, notwithstanding some bizarre allocations of chassis types by the Ministry of War Transport. Yorkshire Woollen's experience of Gardner-engined Guy Arabs led to their becoming a regular purchase after the war, and a considerable number also joined the West Riding fleet. South Yorkshire's very first 'deckers were utility Daimlers, J. Bullock & Sons was amongst the favoured few who also received Bedford OWB saloons, but West Yorks Road Car only gained a handful of Bristol K6As.

Amongst the municipalities, Bradford's fleet was transformed by hordes of wartime-bodied buses and trolleybuses, the former mostly Daimlers, but with a trio of very box-like Guys thrown in for good measure, and Leeds belatedly received Daimlers of utility outline after a five-year interval without new stock.

The ending of hostilities brought little respite, and until replacements could catch up with six years arrears of purchasing in many fleets, in an era of chronic shortages and escalating costs, many veterans had to remain in service well beyond their intended life.

Top left:
A Thornbury-built car of 1926, outward bound Bradford 48 passes a 1934 trolleybus loading in Victoria Square, in the 'Phoney War' period. Headlamps and destination blinds are masked for the blackout, the latter so effectively that the conductor has not bothered to change it to 'Southfield Lane' or 'Horton Bank Top'! *W. J. Haynes*

Centre left:
A Roe-bodied Leyland Titan TD3 of 1934, Yorkshire Woollen 308 (HD 5351) already looked dated when this early wartime view was taken in Dewsbury. It was amongst the last tramway-replacement buses bought, and therefore had a centre entrance and twin staircases.
Yorkshire Woollen District Transport Co/Courtesy R. Marshall

Below:
Eastern Coach Works highbridge bodies integrated quite well in a largely Roe-bodied fleet, with their close similarity of design. A Leyland TD5, Yorkshire Woollen 455 entered service in 1939, and the difficulties of driving in the blackout can well be imagined from the near-obliteration of head and sidelights.
Yorkshire Woollen District Transport Co/Courtesy R. Marshall

Left:
Whilst West Yorkshire escaped lightly from the Blitz, Leeds suffering worst, on 14 March 1941, it was only in Bradford that PSVs were significantly damaged. This 1938 English Electric-bodied AEC trolleybus obviously had a close call in an October 1940 air-raid.
Bradford Metropolitan Libraries

Below:
Unlike the city's buses, few Leeds trams received wartime liveries. Horsfield 226, here at Meanwood, must have been an early exception judging by the amount of meat hanging in Dewhurst's window, and the tinned foods still on display in the grocer's next door!
E. Thornton

The prototype Middleton Bogie built by Brush in 1933 was often relegated to the Hunslet shuttle because of non-standard lower-powered motors. Still elegant in prewar livery, it stands at Thwaite Gate terminus in 1942, astride the still-wired depot connection which had closed to trams two years earlier.
E. Thornton

A *'Flat Harriet'* (or more unkindly *'Pig Trough'*) on a rush-hour turn in Hall Ings, Bradford, still in wartime livery. Delivered in January 1945, No 498 was one of 15 harsh-riding Duple lowbridge-bodied Daimler CWA6s, heartily disliked by crews and passengers alike, and sold as soon as decently possible, in this case to Nottingham Corporation in 1952. *R. Marshall*

Postwar vehicle shortages caused many weary veterans to soldier on beyond their intended life, but 419 (KY 9124) looked more archaic than most, its peaked-roof English Electric body being *passé* even when new in 1935. *R. F. Mack*

Independent Spirits . . .

Whilst the area-agreement companies rapidly consolidated their territories after 1925, many of their operations were founded on the enterprise of small businesses, some of whom defended their independence so vigorously that even today a few survive. By their very nature the independants were opportunists, and so a fascinating galaxy of vehicles characterised their fleets in the 1920s, when chassis of European and North American origin fought for a place in the market alongside a much greater variety of domestic products than can nowadays be readily imagined. Amongst the more obscure makes were Brockway, Federal, Gotfredson, Maxwell, and Willys-Overland, from the States, Laffly and Berliet from France, Minerva of Belgium, Italy's SPA and Lancia, and our own Bean, Belsize, BAT, Caledon, Churchill, Garner, Napier, Star, AJS, and Palladium; all these, and more, were represented in the region!

The post-1929 depression thinned the ranks of manufacturers (where normal market forces had not already done so), and the 1930 Road Traffic Act wreaked havoc with the more-ephemeral independents, producing a remarkable transformation within a decade. Amongst the survivors were some sizeable operations, West Riding Auto and J. Bullock & Sons (B & S) being the prime examples, but Ledgard, Hanson, Baddeley Bros, G. F. Tate, Kippax, Farsley, and others, were all still engaged on stage work.

On the excursions and tours side there was still much greater fragmentation, and when the war knocked the bottom out of that market, many of the coaches which escaped requisitioning were soon redeployed on contract services to munitions factories, used as auxiliary vehicles by the fire and ambulance services, or loaned to larger operators.

In the five years after 1945, traffic reached an all-time peak, and anything that could be persuaded to stay on the road found ready use. With the availability of new vehicles subject to strict control, many still-serviceable chassis had to be rebodied to extract a few more years life from them, and countless firms up and down the country were eager to redirect their resources to meet the need. Wallace Arnold had deemed it expedient to acquire Wilks & Meade as a coach-building and chassis-reconstructing subsidiary

during the war, for this very purpose, and Woodall Nicholson of Halifax (which still has a fine reputation in the funeral trade for its hearses), also rebuilt or produced new bus and coach bodywork on a small scale for nearly a decade, but there were also others.

At this time there had been mounting concern that all bus operations across the country would be nationalised, and reformed into regional groups akin to the British Road Services organisation on the road haulage side of the industry, and it was probably this potential fate which prompted B & S to sell-out its 170-strong fleet to arch-rival West Riding Automobile in September 1950.

The nationalisation threat soon passed away, only to be replaced by more ominous developments. The ending of fuel rationing was accompanied by several sharp increases in the duty on diesel oil, and a steady increase in real incomes was matched with a growing availability of cars on the home market. The Kippax & District and Farsley Omnibus undertakings soon came under Wallace Arnold control, as did many of the remaining coach operators, this process reaching its most dramatic stage in the fateful month of October 1967, when both Ledgard and West Riding passed into the hands of the Transport Holding Company (ie the nationalised sector). Ledgard's demise was the result of direct acquisition by West Yorkshire Road Car, almost all traces of the former ownership being swept away with near-indecent haste. On the other hand, West Riding has maintained its outward appearance of autonomy, at least to the layman. Ironically, a similar spectre to that which pervaded the industry in the late-1940s was probably the motivation, namely the effect the advent of a regional passenger transport authority was likely to have on the company's prospects; in the event this did not happen locally until 1974. It has also been said that West Riding's costly involvement with such a large number of Guy Wulfrunian buses was a factor in the decision to sell-out.

On a less dramatic scale, Hanson's stage-carriage services passed to Huddersfield Corporation in 1969, and its coaching activities to the newly-formed PTE in 1974, the latter subsequently absorbing Baddeley Brothers' operations around Holmfirth.

Above:
One of a pair of A13-type Leyland 2-tonners supplied in 1925 to Hartley Brothers & Rhodes of Kippax, similar to the Hebble bus illustrated in *Roads & Rails of West Yorkshire*. This pneumatic-tyred pioneer must have given some lively competition to West Riding Auto. The unusual telephone number 'Garforth 58Y5' is noteworthy.
Leyland Vehicles Ltd

Below:
As Ripponden & District opted out of limited stop and stage-carriage services in the mid-1930s, it sensibly modernised serviceable vehicles for their new role. A renumbered Leyland Tiger TS1 of 1928, with an unidentified make of coach body, stands outside the garage which still exists today.   *Ripponden & District Motors Ltd*

Above:
The exotic tradition was continued into postwar years and included a pair of Foden PVFE6 two-stroke-engined models of 1950, fitted with Crellin-Duplex 1½-deck bodies built by Mann Egerton. As almost half the passengers had to sit facing rearwards, in a claustrophobic layout, the design enjoyed a very limited vogue.
Ripponden & District Motors Ltd

Left:
The maroon, yellow, and white livery of this long-lived Kippax & District AEC Regal of 1933 was a welcome antidote to the sombre hues prevalent in Leeds' Central Bus Station in postwar years. The Roe body was a very early example of BET Federation influence rather than the manufacturer's own styling. *R. F. Mack*

Top right:
A 'flying pig' with a chequered career, Dennis Ace AWT 592 of 1935 'kicked-off' with Morley & District of Drighlington, spent 1945 with J. J. Longstaff of Mirfield and a further 18 months with J. Steel of Addingham, before settling down in Lancashire with Hodder Motor Services of Slaidburn for its final 10 years or so. In addition, it had received this 1937 ECW body from Keighley-West Yorkshire's K613 in 1950!   *R. F. Mack*

Centre right:
Built as a stock chassis in 1932, three years elapsed before Karrier Chaser HD 5648 was fitted with Lee 32-seat coachwork to enter the mixed fleet of J. Bragg & Son of Dewsbury. In 1937 it passed with the business to Yorkshire Woollen District, only to be requisitioned in 1940. After many years in police service, it was finally scrapped in 1954.   *W. J. Haynes*

Below:
Duple bodywork predominates in this late-1930s publicity view of Longstaff's fleet. The second vehicle from the right is HD 5326, illustrated with its second body in *Roads & Rails of West Yorkshire*. The others, from left to right are: HD 5967 Bedford WTB (1936); EK 9276, Dennis Lancet/Burlingham (1933); HD 5627, Leyland TS7 (1935); WW 3505, Leyland PLSC (1928) and HD 5968, Bedford WTB (1936).   *J. J. Longstaff & Sons*

Below:
The unexpected could still turn up in Dewsbury in the 1960s and OUP 579, a Sentinel STC4 of 1951, arrived on the scene for four years in December 1961, from Phillips of Glynceiriog, later passing by coincidence to another operator named Phillips, in Shiptonthorpe!
J. J. Longstaff & Sons

Bottom:
The postwar vehicle shortage led to coachbuilding activities by many companies with an ephemeral interest in the craft, but the Tower body on this 1947 Albion PX67 (FWY 171) operated by E. Grange of Guiseley, had classic styling.
R. F. Mack/Courtesy P. Seaword

Top right:
Baddeley Brothers of Holmfirth bought both new and secondhand machines, and here is a 1929 Leyland LT1 Lion with Leyland body, which had served as Scottish Motor Traction's G 38 (SC 4321) until 1939; thinly disguised with a CovRad substitute radiator, it served the bleak moorland routes for 11 years. *J. Morris Bray*

Centre right:
One of two Commers bought new by Baddeley Bros in 1949, this Q4 model was fitted with rare Woodall Nicholson 30-seat coachwork which had more than a passing resemblance to Plaxton's contemporary products.
Woodall Nicholson

Below:
The shared ownership of County Motors (Lepton) Ltd between two BET companies and a major independent (West Riding), led to an interesting vehicle policy. No 85 was one of a pair of 1949 Leyland Tiger PS1s with later Windover coachwork which might have looked more attractive with a concealed radiator. *R. F. Mack*

Above:
West Riding Automobile influence presumably led to the purchase of two Guy Wulfrunians with 75-seat Roe bodies for County Motors in 1961. No 99 is seen when almost new, in Lord Street, Huddersfield, and passed to West Riding's own fleet two years later; it is now preserved in the latter's livery. *Author*

Below:
The 32-seat body built by Ramsden of Liversedge on this Dennis E chassis was very up-to-date for 1927, but a ride from Leeds to London on the roads of the day must have tested the fortitude of passengers. It had entered the fleet two years before the takeover by Ernest Bullock.
South Yorkshire Road Transport

Above:
The reconstituted B&S company maintained earlier vehicle policy until the end of the 1920s, and 95 (HL 4347) was a standard 1929 Leyland Tiger TS2 chassis seen here in Scarborough. However, whilst the bodywork has some Leyland characteristics, its front-end design suggests another, unknown, source. *Leyland Vehicles Ltd*

Below:
The new regime at South Yorkshire soon began to standardise on the Albion marque. The full-size PMA28 model was the initial choice, this example entering service in 1930; the bodybuilder is not known.
Clark Photography, Courtesy Pontefract Museum

Top left:
Meanwhile, 'the opposition' began to diversify widely, and in the same year purchased six different models of chassis, one of which was an AEC Regal 662 model No 114 (HL 4770). It is recorded as having a Plaxton body with canvas folding roof, but the ventilators look very permanent fixtures! *W. J. Haynes*

Centre left:
The sleek Ribble-inspired English Electric coachwork on No 43 (AWR 580) was rather let down by the old-fashioned Albion radiator design on this 1934 PW 67 model. However, the £625 spent in Preston was a good investment, as it gave 20 years service.
Clark Photography, Courtesy Pontefract Museum

Below:
Caught by the camera in West Riding days, B&S No 222 had the distinction of bearing three successive bodies in its 25-year career. A 1938 Leyland Tiger TS8, it started life with a Barnaby coach body, reappeared from the same factory with new coachwork in 1946, and 10 years later inherited this Willowbrook saloon from a 1947 Tiger PS1! *H. W. Peers*

Top:
Leaping into the postwar era, we see a Strachan bodied B&S Daimler CVD6 of 1947 in Leeds, which only lasted five years into the takeover by West Riding in September 1950. Premature structural deterioration was the usual reason for early withdrawal of this bodybuilder's products.
W. J. Haynes

Above:
Only a few months older, No 286 (AHL 696) was amongst the first batch of postwar Leyland Tigers bought. A PS1 model with uncommon Barnaby body, it remained structurally unaltered until withdrawal in 1965, although some of its sisters had been rebuilt as double-deckers nine years earlier.   *R. F. Mack*

. . . and Resolute Rebels

Both Hebble and Ledgard had origins in road haulage operation, dating back to the days of horse and steam traction, although the former was then known by the family name of O. & C. Holdsworth. Likewise, both started their major bus service development in 1924; however, their styles of operation were very different.

Hebble adopted a very pugnacious attitude from the start, literally carving out a compact operating territory from under the noses of the Halifax Watch Committee, who adamantly refused to grant licences in an effort to protect the corporation's tramway undertaking. Although Halifax was the hub of operations, the compelling urge to expand soon led to friction with Huddersfield Corporation also, and the first of many licensing appeals to the Ministry of Transport.

The General Strike of 1926 proved a windfall for the company at a most fortuitous moment in its development, prompting the start of further interurban services to Bradford, Leeds, and Manchester. Although the Manchester journeys had to be curtailed at Rochdale afterwards, the following two years saw extensions across the moors from Hebden Bridge to Burnley, participation in a new Bradford to Huddersfield joint service, and the introduction of a summer daily express operation from Halifax to Blackpool.

By this time 60 buses were running 20 services, and so rapid had expansion been that the first covered garage accommodation had only opened a year earlier. The fleet had started with Leylands, but the first Albions were bought in 1926, and later secondhand acquisitions added several other makes to the fleet.

Quite unexpectedly, the Holdsworth family sold out to the region's two main line railway companies in April 1929, but the ensuing Joint Committee arrangements with Halifax led to the loss of seven services, some buses, and abstraction of 35% of receipts in the JOC area. This spurred Hebble into developing express, contract, and excursion work, and to the purchase of several local coach operators in postwar years. It became a British Electric Traction subsidiary in 1932.

Leyland double-deckers entered the fleet in 1929, remaining the sole choice until the war, but Albions were preferred for saloon and coach duties, until a general switch to AECs occurred after 1945. Exceptionally, a large batch of Leyland Royal Tigers in both bus and coach form arrived in the early 1950s, and there was a later dilution of Fords and Commers. Being small enough to retain a family spirit amongst its staff, and to prove a valuable training ground for BET managers, it was sadly rationalised out of existence by NBC policy, after 1971.

Samuel Ledgard took the contrary path of expanding into less-sensitive areas when building up his stage carriage services, the first being in partnership with existing independents on the Leeds to Otley road in 1924. There followed a series of acquisitions over the following decade, which consolidated his position as the primary operator in and around lower Wharfedale, and also provided a valuable service across this territory between Bradford and Harrogate, together with further excursions and tours business.

On the rolling-stock side, Leylands were the near-universal choice for additions from 1928 to 1940, and again immediately after the war, but a wide assortment entered the fleet through acquisitions. Daimler, Guy, and Bedford utilities were joined by six Foden coaches bought about 1950. The deliberate purchase of secondhand stock, which enthusiasts found so engrossing, started just after the founder's death in 1952, and continued over a 14-year period, the last entering service only months before the company's demise in October 1967. The purchaser, West Yorkshire Road Car, had such a high degree of fleet standardisation at the time, that only 12 Ledgard vehicles were taken into operational stock; even they were eliminated within three years, thus removing most traces of Ledgard's unique character from the area in which it had become a legend in its time.

Above:
All this company's prewar double-deckers were Leylands, the initial batch of four being Titan TD1 models of 1929, with draughty open-staircase lowbridge bodywork. No 69 (CP 7576) toiled up and down Halifax's steep hills for 10 years. *Leyland Vehicles Ltd*

Centre right:
Hebble's single-deck fleet was also an Albion stronghold, six Valkyrie PW65 saloons arriving in 1932 with distinctive Brush bodywork of the style seen here on CP 9833.
R. Marshall/Courtesy L. J. Patch

Bottom right:
Never a firm to waste good assets, Hebble rebodied a pair of inherited LMS Railway Leyland Tiger TS2s in 1934, one of which was illustrated in the author's previous book, in original condition. Northern Counties of Wigan designed the superb new coachwork for them, and 119 (UR 3765) thereby remained quite up to acceptable standards until it made its final journey in 1949. *G. Mitchell Collection*

Above:
Overshadowed by their more striking Weymann-bodied cousins were some 1947-built AEC Regal 0662 models; their 32-seat Roe bodies looked more like Willowbrook products. *D. Akrigg*

Below:
Delivered as war broke out, 161 (JX 7991) was an ECW lowbridge-bodied Leyland TD5, whose characteristic engine noise when climbing up to Shelf or Queensbury is still affectionately remembered by older enthusiasts. Note the footplate behind the rear wheelarch, for access to the nearside Clayton destination box.
R. Marshall/Courtesy L. J. Patch

Top left:

Willowbrook did in fact provide lowbridge bodywork for a batch of AEC Regent Mk III models in 1952. Whilst the upper-deck front window treatment spoilt the forward view for passengers, they were very reliable buses, well-liked by drivers and engineering staff. *L. J. Patch*

Centre left:

The same coachbuilder had also won the contract for Hebble's first underfloor-engined saloons, 7ft 6in-wide Leyland PSU1/11 Royal Tigers delivered in 1951. Initially they had operated in a mainly-cream livery, being primarily used on express and private hire duties. *L. J. Patch*

Below:

Ledgard's early standardisation on the Leyland Lion as the backbone of its stage-carriage fleet was a wise choice; this resplendent PLSC1 model was the first of the line, entering service in August 1926 for 12 years duty.
Leyland Vehicles Ltd

Top:
Leyland Titan TD4 EUG 123 was the sole double-decker purchased between 1935 and 1939. Nominally owned by Cream Bus, it is appropriately seen at the outer end of the Ilkley-Guiseley-Leeds route. The standard Leyland body of 1937 looked rather 'boxy' in lowbridge form *R. F. Mack*

Above:
Only a decade had elapsed when this Tiger TS7 with English Electric body arrived on the scene. Of pure Ribble styling, it rubbed shoulders with PLSC Lions for at least six years, and was not withdrawn until 1957. *GEC Traction*

Top right:
The first new double-deckers for five years arrived in 1957, comprising six AEC Regent Vs, and a lone Daimler CVG6 with Burlingham body. The latter is seen in City Square, Leeds, in its last month of Ledgard service, but it was one of the select few to run under the West Yorkshire Road Car banner a little while longer.   *Author*

Centre right:
Among the more exotic additions in the massive 1963 intake of secondhand stock were eight Guy Arab LUF models with Picktree 35-seat bodies. They had been built in 1954 and came from the Northern General fleet, their lives being cut short by the Ledgard sale.   *C. Jones*

Below:
Not a PSV rally, just part of the 1967 rush-hour scene, as two Ledgards, a Road Car Lodekka, and a Bradford trolley proceed in line-astern up Little Horton Lane. The Leyland-bodied PD1A had come from Preston in 1961, whilst the ex-London RTL (LLU 853) was unable to give 12 months service before the company's demise.   *Author*

9

Automobiles, Buses, Road Cars!

The Yorkshire (West Riding) Electric Tramways had a very astute board of directors, which came to terms with the limitations of its undertaking at a crucial period in the development of the motorbus, into which it diversified with considerable vigour. With an incredible degree of standardisation for the era, they purchased over 100 Bristols within three years of commencing bus operation in 1922, and continued to patronise that firm's products in diminishing numbers, until a total switch to Leyland purchases was accomplished 11 years later. The latter then remained sole supplier right through to 1942, when wartime difficulties enforced a change to Guys.

Only eight relatively-small operators were taken over in prewar days, all in the 1930s, and so there was little dilution of fleet standards then. The acquisition of the B & S business in 1950 completely altered this picture, adding an exotic assortment of rolling-stock. The longevity always associated with West Riding's vehicles maintained interest through the next two decades, heightened by much rebodying and rebuilding, and the retention of the last prewar buses as late as 1962. Additionally, some off-beat purchases like a pair of Seddons, and some rare 30ft-long Leyland Tigers, in the early 1950s, and much later, Daimler Roadliners and AEC Swifts, kept the younger enthusiast intrigued, but all were overshadowed by the largest fleet of Guy Wulfrunians in the country, built up from 1959 onwards. When they were prematurely withdrawn, an assortment of secondhand Bristol Lodekkas, plus a few relatively-new Halifax Dennis Lolines, kept everyone guessing as to where the next purchases would come from.

Whilst the Yorkshire (Woollen District) Electric Tramways also had problems to contend with in the early 1920s, unbridled bus competition was not amongst them, generally speaking. Furthermore, it was almost encircled by other substantial operators, and could not initially get licences to serve desirable interurban objectives with buses. Operations therefore developed much more slowly than those in West Riding's territory, there being few independents ripe for acquisition.

BET vehicle policy was very closely adhered to throughout the existence of that Group (to 1968), and Leylands were almost exclusively purchased, apart from a short interlude with Dennis E-types in the mid-1920s, until Guys became imperative during the war. Brush bodywork was the primary choice in the 1920s, with Roe products in the majority during the following decade. The only radical departure was some mid-1930s Weymann coachwork of unconventional styling for its day. After the war, an urgent need to replace the single-deck fleet produced an unfortunate legacy of obsolete half-cab saloons within a very short time, but this was dealt with by rebodying a number as double-deckers, and extending some others for express summer-relief work, where conductors were not essential. Although being one of the very few operators to purchase a Royal Tiger saloon before buying Leyland Olympics, AECs became standard from 1955 until a reversion to Leylands occurred seven years later, with a subsequent admixture of Daimler Fleetlines. During the early-1950s some long-term hires were indulged in, whilst wartime Guys were rebodied, and a vehicle crisis after 1968 led to some surprising secondhand acquisitions, which included AEC Bridgemasters from South Wales Transport, Leyland Titans and Atlanteans from Sheffield JOC, and Bristol KSWs.

West Yorkshire Road Car had grown out of a differing more-rural environment, less friction had occurred with municipal operators, and it was primarily an empire of acquisitions; some were of significant size, like Premier Transport, Blythe & Berwick, and Keighley Brothers. It therefore had a very mixed fleet until the mid-1930s, although standardisation firmly applied to new purchases saw policies which had started with Tilling-Stevens in the previous decade, including Leylands from 1928 to 1934, half-hearted dalliance with Dennis chassis from 1932 to 1938, and culminated in near-total dedication to the Bristol marque, after a hesitant start in 1934. West Yorkshire was noteworthy, of course, for the special arrangements reached with Keighley and York Corporations in 1932 and 1934, respectively, which resulted in the formation of semi-autonomous fleets in those areas, but on which the dead hand of conformity descended as regards rolling-stock and liveries.

In the decade or so after 1945, the Bristol/ECW commitment became so strong that relief was afforded only by a prototype Lodekka, a couple of outlandish livery variations on a pair of KSWs used on limited-stop work, the rebuilt JO5G saloon, a few Bedfords and Beadles, late examples of half-cab LLs and LWLs, and the drawn-out demise of bible indicators. Not long before the latter disappeared, the few Ledgard buses taken into active stock provided a final flutter of interest, a far cry from the halcyon days of the 1920s and 1930s for the older rolling-stock enthusiast.

Below:
The quartet of 1934-built Titan TD3s were the first of many
prewar Leylands equipped with Lysholm-Smith
torque-convertors, and had been ordered by Hartley Bros &
Rhodes. No 371 had a brief career by West Riding standards,
being withdrawn as early as 1945.   *Leyland Vehicles Ltd*

Bottom:
On the other hand, the late-1930s Leyland Tigers had very
long lives, No 440 working from 1936 to 1957. This
Roe-bodied TS7 is seen in Doncaster, but similar vehicles
were an everyday sight in Leeds and Wakefield to the end of
their days.   *R. Marshall*

WEST RIDING

ASKERN
DONCASTER
ASKERN
HL 7514

Top left:
Postwar fleet replacement only got under way as late as 1948, when a massive influx of new rolling-stock included six AEC Regal Mk IIIs like 647, with preselector gearboxes, and stumpy 32-seat Roe bodies. Their appearance nowadays would raise many an eyebrow, but throughout most of their 18-year lives they were outclassed by more-interesting older buses.
L. W. Rowe

Centre left:
Eighteen Roe-bodied Leyland Tigers arrived as late as 1952, in both bus and coach versions, and were all 8ft wide and 30ft long. The six PS2/13A coaches were rare specimens, which usually eluded photographers, but one of each type has been saved for preservation.
P. J. Relf

Below:
The last half-cab Leyland 'deckers purchased were 10 PD2/22s which came in 1954 and were fitted with Roe lowbridge bodies of a style soon to become commonplace on more-numerous Mark IV Guy Arabs. Many displays on one-piece destination screens did not include route numbers, which must have been confusing to casual passengers unfamiliar with the company's complex route pattern. *Author*

Above:
To the end of its independent existence, unusual additions were made to the fleet, and the 1966 surprise was the arrival of 10 Daimler rear-engined SRC6 saloons bodied by Plaxton. Damned by unreliable Cummins engines like others of their breed, 130 and its sisters were withdrawn after only seven years use.   *C. Jones*

Centre right:
Yorkshire Woollen's double-deckers were usually bodied by Roe in prewar days, and so the advent of nine tram-replacement Leyland TD3s with well-styled 48-seat Weymann bodies in 1933 was a pleasant surprise. No 269 (HD 5041) disappeared with the rest of its brethren in 1949.
Yorkshire Woollen District Transport/Courtesy R. Marshall

Bottom right:
The company remained a faithful devotee of BET Federation designs for saloons from 1932, however, which meant a variety of sources but consistency of styling. In 1935 Roe had the bodywork contract, some being painted in overall cream for express work. No 357 enjoyed a twilight existence with Northern General from 1949 to 1956.
Leyland Vehicles Ltd

Top left:
Ten prewar Tigers were given a further lease of life in 1952, their running units being incorporated in coaches built by Beadle of Dartford. No 753 was named *Yorkshire Dragoon*, and looks half as wide again as the Ribble Royal Tiger alongside, at Blackpool's Coliseum coach station.
H. W. Peers

Centre left:
Such was the demand for new vehicles after the war, that YWD was only able to obtain 15 buses in 1947, all being Guy Arab IIIs with Northern Coachbuilder's bodies, their projecting indicators being reminiscent of prewar practice. The dreary post-1952 all-red livery had already blighted 536 when this photo was taken.   *R. Marshall*

Below:
New postwar coaches came only in 1948, with the delivery of just six Duple-bodied Leyland PS1s, although other difficulties were significantly eased by the arrival of 90 buses. No 636 leaves the spartan facilities of Wellington Street coach station, Leeds, bound for Liverpool, whilst a West Yorks L6B of the same vintage, in dual-purpose livery, takes a rest.   *R. F. Mack*

Top right:
The years 1953 and 1954 saw no new vehicles purchased, and a major rebodying programme for the utility Guys was only made possible by hiring from other companies. Hence this 1945 Ribble Roe-bodied Guy (ACK 873) looking quite at home outside Swinegate tram depot, on a Leeds to Dewsbury service. *Author*

Centre right:
A marked change in policy brought AEC Regent Vs into the fleet from 1958, the most attractive being a 1961 batch with Northern Counties 80-seat bodies. Some went to Hong Kong after withdrawal 10 years later, but not No 97 (originally 850), seen here in City Square, Leeds. Note the anti-PTE poster on the side. *Author*

Below:
The Tilling-Stevens era died hard with West Yorkshire, the B49A model in the foreground (No 718) arriving as late as 1932. Withdrawn after only seven years, it spent the war with Bristol Tramways. Behind is No 273, a B10A2 of 1930, which became an evacuee in County Durham. Although allegedly fitted with Eastern Counties and Roe bodies respectively, 718 looks like the Roe product! *W. J. Haynes*

Top left:
Great reliance was placed on rebodied Leyland Tigers for coach services in the late 1930s. This magnificent 1936 Eastern Counties specimen (561, WW 9794) had been placed on a 1929 TS2 chassis, originally numbered 511, ran on producer gas in 1943/4 and, after 18 months hibernation, served the company again from 1946 to 1949.
W. J. Haynes

Centre left:
Looking incredibly antique by the end of their days, ECW-bodied Bristol L5Gs like SG49 and SG82 of 1939/40 could be seen in service until 1960, and had been used to duplicate express services well into the 1950s. *Author*

Below:
A similar 1937 Bristol JO5G had its ECW half-cab body transformed from 32 to 44-seat capacity by the Company in 1952, with one-man-operation as the spur. It remained unique, however, until withdrawal five years later; 965 (BWT 760) is seen in Vicar Lane, Leeds. *R. F. Mack*

Top right:
In 1934/5 the company bought many of the new Bristol GO5G chassis, No 312 being one of the earliest examples. All but the initial pair received Eastern Counties bodywork, mostly of lowbridge layout, and they all lasted into the early-1950s. Their original colour scheme had suited them much better than this postwar Tilling Group livery.
R. F. Mack/Courtesy West Yorkshire Information Service

Centre right:
Bristol K6G chassis began to arrive in 1937, and many were rebuilt with standard ECW bodies and postwar pattern radiators. This made them indistinguishable from newly-delivered stock, and extended their lives to the 1960s. DG9 is on a race day special, together with Lodekka DX45 of 1956. *R. F. Mack,/Courtesy J. F. Gill*

Below:
The 10 Bristol MW5Gs delivered in 1959 had dual-purpose seating and were soon repainted into more-attractive non-standard liveries, until demoted to bus work. EUG 76 is seen leaving Blackpool on a Yorkshire Pool service in 1963, and passed to Lincolnshire Road Car eight years later.
Author

10

Falling From Grace

In the early postwar period the Leeds tramway undertaking still held powers to extend to the Seacroft estate and plans for city-centre subways in the pending tray, together with an ex-Sunderland 1931 single-deck bogie car tucked in a corner of Kirstall Road Works, which, with suitable adaptation, was intended as a trial vehicle for the latter scheme.

The immediate problem, however, was to rehabilitate the existing system after the enforced neglect of track and rolling-stock maintenance since 1939. Traffic congestion caused by other vehicles, and the long-outstanding 'Pivotal' problem, were also giving the trams a worse press than they really deserved, considering the long stretches of reserved track on some routes, and the stalwart service being given by the Horsfields and Middleton Bogies. Artificially low fares producing inadequate revenue, and the growing divergence in capital costs and convergence of running costs between trams and buses, provided fertile ground for those who wished to make the subject a political issue on short-term criteria.

Unwisely, Vane Morland, the general manager, insisted on unconventional features for a postwar car specification, which the few tramcar builders left around were unwilling to contemplate, at acceptable tendering prices, and so recourse had to be made to more secondhand purchases, initially from Manchester and Southampton, subsequently from London. The first two batches of cars, long past their prime, did nothing to popularise the system, and merely provided further ammunition to its adversaries. The Feltham cars from London Transport were much more up-to-date in concept, but hamstrung in performance through being interspersed with handbraked veterans of the 1920s, and noisy when running over street track, most of which had been corrugated by the Pivotals.

The particular misfortune of the trams was that they had been able to stay in service with minimal attention, when much newer buses had required costly reconstruction or replacement at the end of the war. Accordingly, almost 200 new buses had been purchased by 1950, highlighting the difference in standards between the two forms of transport. There had been a total lack of policy with regard to the tramways whilst the bus problem had been dealt with, and the inflation which had intervened made it politically unacceptable to face the huge investment needed to modernise the system. Worse still, their chief protagonist, in the shape of W. Vane Morland, had retired, and all but the most trivial day-to-day matters appeared to fall within the political arena, namely in the hands of the transport committee and its chairman, rather than the chief officers of the undertaking.

Surprisingly, the Middleton to Belle Isle link had been opened in this period of uncertainty, using redundant tracks from recently-closed routes, and two new single-deck cars had been sanctioned to ascertain the best types of electrical and mechanical equipment for the subway services. However, by the time they entered service in mid-1953, the local political situation had just determined the fate of the system, which was to be closed within 10 years. In the event, the programme was speeded up so that the last cars ran on 7 November 1959, along York Road.

The principal features of some of the intermediate closures had been the elimination of many arbitrary cross-city tram links by even stranger bus connections (on pure expediency rather than passenger need), the swamping of newly-converted routes, for a few weeks only, by the replacing buses, before a permanent reduction in frequencies, and the use of resurrected prewar vehicles which had been in store for considerable periods, in the early stages of the programme.

Above:
The ex-Hull cars in Leeds were transformed in appearance, if not performance, by the standard fleet colours, quickly applied after 1945. No 472 had arrived in 1942, and is seen alongside Swinegate depot being loaded with the removable posts used for the 'football special' queue in Concordia Street.   *A. D. Packer*

Below:
The postwar search for economy resulted in gradual simplification of the ornate liveries, but 1926 Brush-built 'Chamberlain' No 31 looks attractive as it stands on Easterly Road spur in a transitional blue and white paint scheme, still with its Pivotal trucks. Behind stands 'Beeston Air Brake' 387, which has lost only the white paint from its rocker panel.   *A. D. Packer*

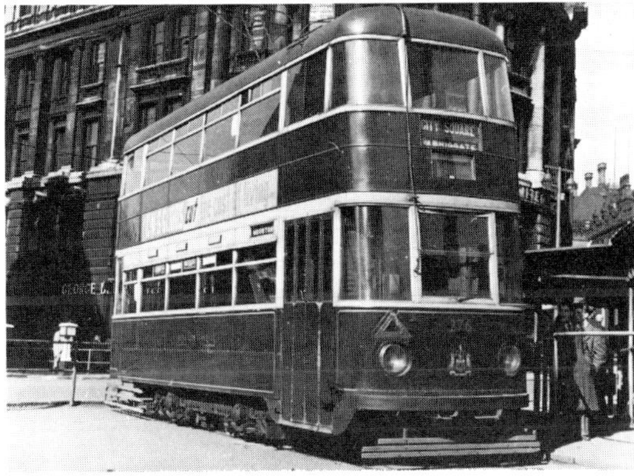

Above:
Special liveries and decorated cars had a long tradition in the city, lasting to 1955. Brush-built Horsfield 230 of 1931, caught in traffic at Harehills Parade, must have been a welcome sight in 1945 after years of austerity and shabby paintwork. *D. W. K. Jones*

Centre left:
False hopes were raised by the appearance of car 276 from Kirkstall Road Works in 1948, the only double-decker built new after the war. Seen in City Square on the vestigial remains of the Infirmary Street line, it soon received the new red and cream livery, and had its three-piece blinds replaced by single screens. *W. J. Wyse*

Bottom left:
'Here today and gone tomorrow' would be a fitting epitaph to the ex-Southampton cars, only a percentage of those bought in 1949 actually entering service, for four years at maximum. Car 290 was the first of the series, hence the pale-blue and cream livery. The white bands on the trees in Street Lane are a relic of the wartime blackout regulations. *A. D. Packer*

Top:
A battered Feltham (501) using the Harehills Lane crossover on York Road delays Horsfields 189 and 191, in a scene redolent of the system's last days. The nearer pair both went to preservation, 189 now running at Crich under its true identity as No 180. The tubular spacer, in lieu of a span wire in the overhead, was typical Leeds practice in the bow-collector era.   *L. W. Rowe*

Above:
A heavy snowfall in February 1958 brought out every car still capable of movement, to keep the reserved track sections open. No 8A had been Dick, Kerr, balcony 198 from 1901 to 1919, whilst its companion (No 6) was an 1899 product, bought from Hull as a works-car conversion in 1943.   *A. D. Packer*

70

11

Tales of the Unexpected

Since the earliest days of motorised transport, operators have adapted, rebuilt, or rebodied vehicles from one shape to another, the primary example being the very early stratagem of using alternative charabanc bodies on goods chassis, in itself a practice which had started in the horse-and-cart era.

As the passenger side of the industry developed between the wars, a number of factors caused operators to rebuild vehicles, sometimes drastically. Several quantum leaps in design or fashion occurred which made perfectly-serviceable machines obsolete almost overnight; secondly, some independents disposed of stage-carriage services, but continued to run tours and excursions, and thirdly, although an eight-year life was still the conventional assumption for buses and coaches, in the late 1930s heavyweight chassis were proving themselves capable of giving much longer service. On the other hand, an unwise choice of chassis could result in perfectly serviceable bodies being wasted.

Some undertakings were confirmed rebuilders, West Yorkshire Road Car perhaps being the leading prewar exponent in the region, finding early petrol-engined Leyland Tigers suitable candidates for new express coach bodies in the mid-1930s. When Ripponden & District gave up its stage and express services in 1934/6, it was left with a number of saloons which had been perfectly adequate for such duties when built, but did not accord with the vogue for streamlined shapes coming into fashion for excursion work, and therefore disguised them most effectively with new coachwork as the illustrations show. Huddersfield had to withdraw prematurely some late-model Karriers in the early 1930s, and transferred their Hall Lewis double-deck bodies to new AEC Regents.

Whilst there were some instances of prewar buses being refitted with utility bodies (eg B & S, West Riding, Leeds, and Bradford), it was in postwar days when the greatest amount of rehabilitation occurred. Like Leeds City Transport with its Daimlers, West Riding Auto even placed a few prewar Roe bodies on Guy chassis. However, Yorkshire Woollen went in for the largest programme of fitting brand new bodies to wartime Guys. West Yorkshire Road Car had very few wartime buses, but rehabilitated many prewar Bristol Ks to the point where they were indistinguishable from new products of the 1946-50 period, apart from their registration marks. Most had ECW bodies, but a few were bodied by Roe to a design closely resembling late-prewar Eastern Coachworks styling, and a few for the York-West Yorkshire fleet were dealt with so extensively, as late as 1955, as to qualify for re-registration. Surprisingly, the contemporary Bristol L5G saloons must have been better constructed, as almost all gave good service to the end of their days, with only a heavy overhaul of their original structure being necessary.

Yorkshire Woollen's interesting saga with surplus saloons, and Leeds' strange rebodying of wartime Daimlers, is briefly referred to in the accompanying captions, but West Riding got involved in complicated transfers, and South Yorkshire Motors, Kippax & District, and Farsley Omnibus all extended lives by rebodying. Hanson's went in for much more dramatic conversions, and Ledgard bought a few prewar vehicles in the 1950s solely to use their bodies as replacements on its own contemporary chassis. Postwar, Huddersfield applied the practice solely to its trolleybuses, where it seemed that an accountant's rather than an engineer's decision lay behind the 12-year life decreed for bodywork. Bradford, of course, became notable for capitalising on short-sighted policies elsewhere, by fitting very uptodate bodies on many of the trolleybuses it acquired secondhand, after having so dealt with most of its own prewar and wartime fleet.

Right:
Looking a little different from its old self, this is actually a Leyland PLC Lioness of 1928, after receiving typically futuristic mid-1930s luxury coachwork by H. V. Burlingham.
Ripponden & District Motors Ltd

Below right:
The operator's own workshops effectively disguised this 1929 Leyland PLSC Lion (45, WW 7619) in the mid-1930s, perhaps borrowing a little inspiration from the manufacturer's contemporary styling.
Clark Photography/Courtesy Pontefract Museum

With 33 rugged utility Guy Arab
chassis allocated to the fleet from
1942 onwards, Yorkshire Woollen
found it worthwhile to rebody most
of them some 10 years later.

Bottom left:
A 1944 Park Royal 56-seater, 494 is
in near-original condition except for
the addition of a route number
display, and was rebodied by Roe in
1953 for a further 12 years
service.   *R. F. Mack*

Right:
The subject of a pre-delivery
exchange with Maidstone & District
for a less-welcome Daimler CWA6,
506 was delivered new to YWD with
a Kent registration. Seen here after
rebodying by Roe in 1952, it lasted
until 1966.   *R. Marshall*

Leeds Corporation had eliminated
most prewar stock from its bus fleet
by 1951 but some surprising
developments were to come!

Left:
The remaining vee-fronted AEC
Regents of the early 1930s were
stored or sold in 1950, this being 153
(ANW 696) of 1934, as T. Burrows of
Wombwell No 73. Some of its
unsold sisters were resurrected for
tramway replacement in 1953/4.
Author

Left:
Meanwhile, a variety of Daimler
CWA6 utilities soldiered on, often in
all day service, this Duple-bodied
machine (98, JUB 601) being
portrayed in its original drab
livery.   *R. Marshall*

Right:
In 1955, some utilities received the 1934/5 Roe bodies from the reactivated AEC Regents, Park Royal-bodied 78 (JUB 578) being a dubious beneficiary of this amazing policy, which only extended its life by two years.   *R. Marshall*

Right and below:
Vehicles of utility outline continued to enter service in Bradford until mid-1946, 705 being a Karrier W/Roe product of a year earlier. Seen in original condition above, it was completely rejuvenated with a new East Lancs 65-seat front-entrance body in 1960, and completed 26 years service.   *R. Marshall/Author*

Above:
Hanson's of Huddersfield went in for more dramatic rebuilding, and 347 (KVH 889) emerged in 1956 with a new Roe 65-seat body on a chassis reworked from two prewar AEC Regals. The front entrance bus behind is 368 of 1962, rebuilt from a 1949 Regent. *L. W. Rowe*

Below:
Obsolete halfcab saloons had become a problem by 1960, and in that year 360 (NCX 543) appeared, which had first seen the light of day as Duple-bodied Regal 9621E saloon 291 of 1949. *Hanson Haulage Ltd*

Changing circumstances in the 1950s led to an over abundance of low-capacity saloons in the Yorkshire Woollen fleet, a problem dealt with in various ways:

Top right:
The 35 Willowbrook-bodied Leyland Tiger PS2/5s of 1950 were lengthened from 32 to 38 seaters, and used on long distance and summer-express relief work for almost 10 years from 1955; here, 724 departs from Blackpool with a returning load of holidaymakers in August 1963, its penultimate season.   *C. Jones*

Centre right:
A handful were further converted in 1963, this time by Roe with Orion-style 63-seat double-deck bodies. No 709 snapped in Wellington Street, Leeds, thereby lasted into the mid 1970s.   *P. J. Relf*

Below:
A few others were sold to Yorkshire Traction in 1963, and also became double-deckers, 798 having been YWD's 714. Rebodied by Northern Counties for a final 10 years service, it looked in fine form arriving in Huddersfield, in this 1967 view.   *Author*

12

Capital Connections

The earliest London-style buses to appear in West Yorkshire were almost certainly Laycock's original double-decker and Todmorden's first Leylands, of the 1905-07 period, followed by Leeds City Tramway's Daimler of 1913. The 1926 AEC single-deckers bought by Bradford, and by Warburton Bros of Headingley for its Otley to Leeds service, were probably the next, if not in appearance then at least in chassis specification, which was closely related to LGOC requirements. Leeds' Dodson-bodied double-decker Dennises of 1929/30 would not have looked out of place on London's streets, either!

One might have thought that the surplus London County Council 'B'-class covered-top trams would have been of interest to the West Riding Tramways in 1917, to replace the losses sustained in its Castleford depot fire. However, another 22 years were to elapse before London cars came north late in 1939, when three HR2s made prematurely redundant by the LPTB's conversion of services north of the Thames to trolleybuses arrived in Leeds, precursors to a larger batch whose transfer was prevented by the outbreak of war.

The next important move was in the opposite direction, a crisis having arisen in London with the damage sustained by its fleet in the opening stages of the Blitz. Halifax, Leeds, Bradford, B & S, West Riding, West Yorkshire, and possibly others, all sent buses south in October 1940, many of which stayed away for about a year. Just a month prior to their departure, one of London's newest buses had visited the area, operating as an AEC demonstrator in Bradford, at least. It was RT19, then intended as representative of the manufacturer's standard postwar design; presumably no one realised at the time just how long the war would last. In stark contrast, 1942 saw the arrival on the regional scene of some of London Transport's oldest buses. These being ex-LGOC short-wheelbase Regents of 1930/1 which helped to eke out the Road Car's fleet of double-decks for over two years, and made possible the conversion of Bradford's Stanningley tram route in October 1942; three of the more-antique-looking variants of the same vintage, built for Thomas Tilling with open staircases, also helped the latter cause, but all were found wanting

on the city's steep gradients and were returned within 12 months.

Provincial bus loans to London were again in the news during 1948/49, primarily involving brand-new Bristols for Tilling Group companies. Whilst West Yorks Road Car escaped this penalty, Leeds 'compensated' by hiring a number of prewar AEC Regents to London Transport. About the same time, Leeds was trying out one of the ex-Metropolitan Electric Tramways 1930 Felthams, which must have surprised more-observant passengers with its high LTE fleet number (2099), as well as its red and white livery, in a sea of blue trams. Eventually 90 more arrived, the last to be rehabilitated not entering service until July 1956, whilst seven were eventually scrapped without working in the city at all. Joining them in December 1951 was ex-LCC Bluebird No 1, a 1933 prototype for a fleet which never materialised because of the policy change against tramways by the newly-formed LPTB, soon after it had been built.

Back to buses, and the arrival of more than a score of London utility Daimlers in the Ledgard fleet from 1952 onwards was quite a shock at the time, for an operator who had always bought new Leylands for double-deck work, given free choice. As they were getting to the end of their second wind, a further surprise occurred in Bradford with the purchase in 1958 of 25 ex-London postwar RTs to replace the last of that city's utilities. Body variations, such as they were on these highly-standardised buses, were well represented, and most gave longer service in the north than in their native haunts. Five years later, with the onset of the full RT-withdrawal programme in London, the Bradford examples were matched by Ledgard acquisitions of later origin, 37 arriving between 1963 and 1967, together with four Leyland variants of the RTL class in Ledgard's final year of operation. Ironically they all disappeared from both fleets at roughly the same time, due to West Yorkshire Road Car's mass withdrawal of Ledgard buses immediately after purchasing the company, and life-expiry of the Bradford contingent.

DMS-class Fleetlines have yet to appear in the region, but there is still plenty of time for that to happen!

Right:
London Transport's ST 182 (GF 7226), a 1930 AEC Regent with LGOC 48-seat body, was amongst eight which appeared on the Road Car scene during the war years. Bradford also had similar vehicles, but West Yorkshire's were soon moved from Leeds depot, to the flatter territory around York.
R. F. Mack/Courtesy West Yorkshire Information Service

Above and left:
By the time the Leeds 1935 Weymann streamliner (201, CNW 902) went on loan to London in 1949 it had become a half-cab, lost its non-standard destination equipment, and presented a sorry contrast to its original pristine condition. *D. W. K. Jones/R. Marshall*

The three London HR2 trams which arrived in Leeds in 1939 looked most attractive in pale-blue and cream, and might have been the forerunners of more had the war not intervened. Car 277 is seen at Hunslet in 1942, and remained in service until the late-1950s.   *E. Thornton*

One either liked the Felthams or hated them, but they certainly improved passenger standards even though they were not used to the best advantage operationally. No 509 pauses at Gipton terminus, resplendent in an experimental red and cream livery of the early 1950s.   *R. Brook*

Left:
Burrows of Wombwell acquired three London utilities about 1952, all of which were rebodied by Burlingham some years later, and survived to be taken over (but not operated) by Yorkshire Traction in 1966. This Daimler CWA6, with its original Duple body, had been LTE D84.   *Author*

Left:
The years 1953 to 1955 saw 23 ex-LTE Daimler CWA6s join the Ledgard fleet, most having Park Royal bodies like HGF 876 seen here in Edward Street, Leeds, which gave six years service.   *Author*

Right:
J. J. Longstaff of Mirfield operated a
Craven-bodied RT from 1958 which
was displaced five years later by
this conventional Park Royal model
(RT 504). Retention of the roof-box
route-number was apparently a
nostalgic whim.   R. F. Mack

Right:
Variety in destination equipment on
the 25 former London AECs
acquired by Bradford in 1958 is a
study in itself, even roof boxes
being used where fitted. RT 415 had
been built in 1947 and gave about
the same length of service in its new
home as in the capital.   C. Jones

Right:
Ledgard's second London phase
was curtailed by the company's
unexpected demise in 1967 and,
sadly, RTL852 did not achieve 12
months service in the West Riding.
Resplendent in fresh paintwork, it
speeds past Bradford's Thornbury
depot in April 1967.   C. Jones

13
Final Flourish

The 1950s were perhaps the most interesting decade of all, for those interested in the trolleybus systems of Huddersfield and Bradford. In the former town, majestic six-wheelers in pristine condition glided with quiet efficiency under immaculate overhead; whilst all the prototypes had disappeared, many prewar trolleys were still in daily use early in the decade, and a policy of rebodying the best of these had been implemented, alternating with new purchases. The closure of the Brighouse route beyond the borough boundary at Fixby in July 1955 was therefore a nasty jolt, only partly offset by the opening of a new branch to Bradley (Keldregate) nine months later.

Surprising as it may now seem, prospects were not so certain for the Bradford system in 1950. Whilst the rebodying programme for prewar vehicles had almost been completed, diesel buses were alleged to be cheaper to operate, and the impending retirement of the general manager (C. R. Tattam) threw a big question mark over continued operation. At this time, most of the corporation's rolling-stock was looking distinctly jaded; it was the high operating speeds and level of service provided (two-minute rush-hour frequencies being commonplace), together with the complex web of overhead in the city centre, which provided the main attractions. Paradoxically, cross-city routeings were represented solely by the Bradford Moor-Cross Flatts service, restored in 1951 after an 11-year interval.

As events turned out, the new manager (C. T. Humpidge) was a firm advocate of electric traction, whilst being equally dedicated to improving the motorbus fleet, and plans for further trolleybus extensions and vehicle rebodying were soon being discussed. After the 1949-50 programme there were no more new vehicles, but astute buying of prematurely-redundant trolleys from other undertakings provided an effective substitute, most being rebodied to a very high standard before re-entering service.

The Humpidge regime brought the system to a new peak of efficiency by 1960, with significant modernisation not only of vehicles but also overhead work, which had been realigned promptly wherever required, to improve flexibility amidst the ever-increasing road traffic. Extensions had been opened to Wibsey in 1955, to Buttershaw and Clayton (Avenue) in 1956, at Eccleshill in 1959, and to Holme Wood in 1960, whilst a new cross-city link had at last been provided in 1957, by linking Eccleshill and St

Enoch's Road Top workings.

With the dawn of the 1960s, economic forces were relentlessly stacking-up against trolleybus operation. There was also an illogical but growing public feeling that it was an outmoded form of public transport, particularly after London's total commitment to the diesel bus on very insubstantial criteria.

Huddersfield's April 1960 decision to substitute motorbuses on the remaining extra-territorial services sounded the death-knell for its system, by destroying its integrity, a policy officially denied at first, and followed by the rebodying of 12 more early-postwar vehicles. The rundown was carried out in a sensible manner, however; overhead wire layouts were readily altered when road schemes were implemented, and maintenance kept to high standards until the final days. The last services, from Waterloo to Lindley and Outlane, succumbed on 13 July 1968.

Preparations to celebrate the Golden Jubilee of trolleybus operation in Bradford in 1961 seemed to augur well, until it became known that C. T. Humpidge was to move to Sheffield. Times had changed to the extent that his successor, Mr J. C. Wake, had little experience of electric traction, and was a confirmed motorbus advocate. His appointment coinciding with a bout of perennial hesitation on the part of the transport committee, redevelopment in the city centre was a convenient pretext to clinch the anti-trolleybus case on narrow cost grounds, without regard to its particular suitability to Bradford's uncompromising terrain.

The closure of services traversing Forster Square turned the remainder into poor relations, and almost cut the system in two. Within 18 months, J. C. Wake departed to supervise Nottingham's abandonment, but the psychological damage had been done, and his more sympathetically-inclined successor could only prevent stay of execution until vehicles were financially written-off. There was even one more cross-city connection, of the Thornbury and Thornton routes, as late as March 1965, but by then four services had become casualties.

Within two years, official pronouncements of final closure were made, yet major overhead layout changes in the city centre to accord with the redeveloping street pattern occurring in the interim were on a scale that far-eclipsed the Forster Square requirements, which had been the original catalyst. Normal services finally ran on 24 March 1972, to Duckworth Lane, Thornton, and Thornbury, the very last in the UK.

Top:
Most of Huddersfield's early-postwar Park Royal-bodied Sunbeam MS2s, badged as Karriers, were rebodied within 10 years (like 577 behind). However, 544 (CVH 744) remained unaltered until 1964 withdrawal, although signs of structural weakness can be detected in this view taken three years earlier. *C. Jones*

Above:
The prewar three-window styling of the upper deck had been perpetuated in the 1947-49 deliveries and, in conjunction with their box-like shape, helped to give the false impression that they were 8ft wide. Only a handful of unrebodied examples were given the newer two-piece indicator layout, towards the end of their careers.
L. W. Rowe

Above:
Although Huddersfield's trolleys expired before their Bradford cousins, new vehicles appeared in the former fleet at a much later date. No 619 was a BUT 9641T, with 72-seat East Lancashire body, of the penultimate batch delivered in 1956. *Author*

Below:
Utility-bodied trolleys could be seen in Bradford to a relatively late date, and No 612 was snapped in Tyrrel Street just seven months before retirement in December 1958. It had notched up 24 years service, being an AEC 661T with 1944 Brush bodywork, which had originally been an English Electric 60-seater. *Author*

Secondhand bargains included eight BUT 9611Ts with 63-seat East Lancashire bodies, built in 1950 for St Helens and acquired eight years later. The crew of 795 take a break by the prominent shelter masquerading as '89 Hall Ings', while a slightly newer Regent III, also East Lancs-bodied, pulls away on the joint service to Leeds.   *Author*

Starting the evening run-out from Thornbury on 21 April 1967, 833 was thirdhand, being a BUT 9611T built in 1949 for Darlington, with an East Lancs body like 795 above. After seven years with the Doncaster fleet from 1952, East Lancs rebodied it for Bradford, where it re-entered service in 1962 for its final nine years.   *C. Jones*

14

Up Hill and Down Dale

In contrast to prewar days, when it had perhaps the most interesting tramway system in the region, Halifax paled into insignificance after the war, against the more interesting scenarios being played out in Bradford, Huddersfield, and Leeds. With its very standardised fleet, this applied with even greater degree to Todmorden, which was a backwater to the enthusiast, although well-maintained Leyland Titans served their community to good effect over the years.

Those who made the effort to visit Halifax about 1950 found a bustling town served largely by half-cab AEC Regents and Regals dating from about 1938 onwards, and also some postwar Leyland-bodied PD2s bought for comparison. The prewar buses were being rapidly phased out, and Park Royal bodywork of an uncommon design was fitted to most of the postwar Regents, although some were Roe products, including one or two examples on London RT-type chassis.

Adequate engine power had always been a problem for the town's buses, and the Daimler CD650 model of 125bhp displayed at the 1950 Commercial Motor Show appeared to be the answer, particularly with the added benefit of power-assisted steering; accordingly, six were added to the corporation fleet in 1951. Their inherent vices outweighing their advantages, they were followed by more Regents, and then some conventional 'tin-fronted' Daimler CVG6s with smart Roe bodies, distinguished as the CD650s had been by an enlarged Ribble-style front destination aperture. Thereafter, there was vacillation between Leyland Royal Tiger Worldmasters (disguised under run-of-the-mill BET-style bodies), Leopards, Regent Vs, Leyland Titans, and even five Dennis Lolines, before Daimler Fleetlines became the standard choice after 1966 (including some single-deck versions). The scene had been enlivened by some 1963 Albion Nimbuses (or *Nimbi*?), and then some secondhand AEC Monocoaches and Reliances, the latter soon being rebodied to full coach-standards for an expansion into long-distance private-hire work. Finally, new Reliances, Seddons, and then more Leopards, entered the single-deck fleet.

Huddersfield Corporation did not operate any motorbuses from 1930 to 1962, when the trolleybus conversion scheme first involved internal services, but the JOC had remained very faithful to AECs right through from petrol-engined Regents of the early-1930s to the last Regent V models bought in 1962, except for the lowbridge wartime Daimlers, and a pair of 1959 Mark IV Guy Arabs. The early postwar switch to Daimler saloons, and then Guy underfloor-engined models, was rectified by the purchase of AEC Reliances from 1956 to 1963, apart from a couple of Leyland Leopards bought in 1961, two much-later AEC Swifts, and then more Reliances in 1969, before Seddons became the single-deck preference in 1970.

The corporation asserted its independence in vehicle matters by buying Leyland Titans as its first double-deck diesels in 1961. This was emulated by the JOC two years later, but then both sections of the fleet became Daimler addicts, initially with half-cabs, and then with rear-engined Fleetlines from 1967. For the first few years of renewed motorbus operation, corporation buses were painted in the trolleybus style, but simplification of liveries later resulted in some half-cabs having completely cream fronts, but red sides, without the pleasing curves in the livery on the leading side bays to ease the transition from one predominant colour to the other; the effect was quite bizarre!

Following the 1968 Transport Act, the railway interest in the JOC was transferred to a subsidiary of the newly-formed National Bus Company, which soon disposed of it to the corporation, and so the previous distinction between the two fleets in the town ceased to apply. In the Halifax area a similar, but not identical, amalgamation occurred a little later, with the disappearance of Hebble from the stage-carriage scene to become, for a final two years, merely the coaching unit for Yorkshire Woollen and West Riding Auto, under an NBC reorganisation in 1971. In that same year, the Halifax JOC fleet was merged with that of Todmorden, also absorbing Hebble's local services, and was renamed the Calderdale JOC. The corporation fleet remained separate, but the Halifax livery spread to all the vehicles involved, and thus it could be seen at last in central Bradford on buses running a new jointly-worked service, an aspiration so often held, that 'Halifax' had been added to the destination screens of some Bradford buses in earlier years!

Todmorden JOC apparently lost interest in bus purchase not long before Leyland's cessation of bodybuilding in 1954, and all-Leyland Titan PD2/12 No 27 (KWX 19) was the last double-decker purchased; 10 years were to elapse before the next acquisition in 1961. The Corporation and British Railways emblems can just be discerned on the side panels. *L. W. Rowe*

Its centre bays visibly sagging, Halifax JOC 381 was a 1950 AEC Regent 9612E, with the undertaking's unusual 'spindly' style of Park Royal body. 'Which "Steep Lane"?' the intending passenger might well ask, given Halifax's hilly terrain; inclinometers and horizon-level indicators might well have been the most useful cab instruments! *L. W. Rowe*

Right:
Overpowering in aspect were the unusual 10.6-litre Daimler CD650s with East Lancashire bodies, bought by Halifax in 1951. However, their superior engine performance was negated by high fuel consumption and erratic braking, resulting in early retirement. *R. F. Mack*

Right:
During a period of changing policy, Halifax bought a final batch of AECs in 1960 for both sections of the fleet. They were Regent V models whose uninspiring Metro-Cammell Orion bodies were relieved by the attractive orange, green, and cream livery. Four JOC examples survived into PTE ownership, but the remainder had been sold by 1974. *L. W. Rowe*

Left:
The four-bay Park Royal bodies on Huddersfield's early postwar AEC Regents looked more substantial and up-to-date than the Halifax counterparts which they closely resembled. No 152 was a 1948 delivery, relegated to relief duties when this view was taken in 1961. *C. Jones*

Left:
Lowbridge bodywork was required until quite a recent date for a number of services, and a 1954 East Lancashire 58-seat example is seen here on an AEC Regent III 9613E chassis, in Byram Street.
L. W. Rowe

Left:
AEC Regent V chassis with exposed radiators were comparatively rare, but Huddersfield rated practicality higher than fashionable trends, as long as possible. This 1958 D2RA model was complemented by a sleek 65-seat Roe highbridge body, and was transferred to the Bradford District soon after PTE formation in 1974. *Author*

Above:
Huddersfield made a surprise reversion to Guy chassis after a lapse of 30 years, in opting for the UF model with Gardner engine and Guy bodywork for its initial underfloor-engined saloons in the early-1950s. The legal lettering on No 3 of 1954 shows it to be owned by the British Railways Board, in this 1967 view. *C. Jones*

Centre right:
When trolleybus conversion got under way in the 1960s, the replacing corporation-owned diesel buses retained the cream fronts of their predecessors. The Roe-bodied Leyland PD3A/2s of 1961/2 looked particularly attractive in this livery scheme. *Author*

Bottom right:
Neepsend 70-seat bodywork was fitted to this corporation-owned 1966 Daimler CVG6LX with Manchester-style glass fibre bonnet, but it had the indicator layout hitherto used on the JOC fleet. In the background, a Roe-bodied contemporary in Joint Committee livery is leaving Buxton Road to enter the former roundabout at Manchester Road/Chapel Hill junction.
C. Jones

15

Poles Apart?

The need for new buses in Leeds after the war was so great that recourse was made to three other manufacturers for 56 chassis, before the first deliveries arrived in 1947 from AEC, the preferred supplier. A further 90 were bought from Crossley, Daimler, and Leyland, up to 1950, eliminating most prewar stock, and so the enthusiast's casual assumption that the city was overrun by Roe-bodied Regents was then somewhat wide of the mark.

By 1950, the only prewar buses to have steady all-day employment were the Leyland Tiger saloons, toiling along their undulating cross-suburban route between Wortley and Harehills, with occasional forays to Long Causeway. As if to signify this change in fortunes, the fleet assumed a green mantle in place of the sombre shades of blue previously worn, although the latter remained to distinguish a clutch of prewar Regents permanently used on a contract to Skelton Grange power station.

Across in Bradford, Roe bodywork continued to be conspicuous by its total absence from a motorbus scene more dominated by utilities than in Leeds, until the mid-1950s; the same range of post-1940 chassis was in evidence, in differing proportions, with the addition of three Guys. Prewar English Electric and Weymann-bodied AECs and Daimlers still abounded, all looking very much the worse for wear; they were finally eliminated by the arrival of 40 'tin-fronted' Regent 111s from East Lancashire's works in 1952/53.

Shapely Northern Coachbuilders styling had graced the first normal postwar buses, AECs of 1947/8, and a 1949 contract on Daimler chassis had uniquely gone to Barnard. Bradford was not disadvantaged by a bus station with restricted clearances, and so their Crossleys, Leylands, and Weymann-bodied AECs, of the 1948-50 period, were 8ft wide: Only some 1948 Brush-bodied Daimlers were identical to their Leeds cousins in all but livery.

After the 1953 AECs, six years elapsed before there were more new double-deckers, in the form of 70-seat forward-entrance AEC Regent Vs which arrived in successive batches until 1964. Incidentally, a pair of Roe-bodied AEC Reliances which had despatched the 1936 Regals to the scrapyard at the ripe old age of 22, were put to better use by appearing regularly in normal service, and became remarkable for the livery variations they bore.

Meanwhile, nothing untoward had occurred in Leeds until 1953, but the following two years produced at least three major surprises. Firstly, the withdrawal of the Bramley and Kirkstall trams unleashed prewar AEC Regents dating back to 1934 onto the streets again, and so the vee-fronted Roe bodies saw further employment after three to four years in store; how their replacement four years earlier had been justified to the transport committee, if they were still capable of all-day service, makes interesting speculation! Secondly, the prewar Tigers were at last granted retirement, to be replaced by eight 'crush-loader' saloons of ungainly appearance, with masterly indecision mounted on three different makes of chassis. Lastly, the oldest AECs disappeared after a short spell, but seven of their bodies had a further reincarnation on some 1945/46 Daimlers for a final couple of years, at which time the last prewar Regents were also withdrawn. The unusual practice of replacing normal interior lighting with coloured bulbs, in the pre-Christmas period each year, ceased about the same time.

After that, the fleet became noteworthy mainly for very late purchases of 7ft 6in-wide buses, of Regent Vs with exposed radiators, and a renewed interest in saloons, used particularly on new limited-stop 'Fastaway' services in the late 1960s, as well as on a very infrequent service around the Outer Ring Road. The final departure from convention must surely have been the purchase of five Mercedes-Benz minibuses in 1970, for a shopper's service in the city!

Almost exactly five years after Daimlers had disappeared from Bradford, a Fleetline demonstrator was tried out in July 1964. With excessive caution, it was later announced that 15 would be ordered, but together with 15 half-cab CVG6 models. They all arrived in 1966/7, accompanied by equivalent numbers of the corresponding Leyland types, so no chances were being taken!

A final batch of Leyland Titans in 1968 was distinguished by Alexander bodies. A mixture of almost-identical well-styled Alexander and Metro-Cammell bodies had been specified for the first rear-engined buses, the former firm gaining all the business on subsequent deliveries from both chassis manufacturers in the city's final orders of the 1970-72 period, after 10 Marshall-bodied AEC Swifts and Leyland Panthers (five of each!) had represented the total 1969 intake. Probably due to an understandable reluctance to spend money needlessly on behalf of others, no more buses were purchased in the 18 months prior to the formation of the PTE in April 1974!

Top left:
Leeds 701, a DD42/3 model of 1946, carried the Crossley banner in isolation for three years, before 20 more were added to the fleet, but remained the only example of its manufacturer's most characteristic style of bodywork. Initially numbered 27, on the end of the Leyland Tiger TS8 series, it was withdrawn in 1959. *R. Marshall*

Centre left:
Among the more attractive postwar replacements in Bradford were 20 AEC Regent IIIs of 1947/8. They had Northern Coachbuilders bodies, similar to those used to rebody many prewar trolleybuses, and were replaced in the early-1960s. *Author*

Below:
The Leyland PD2/3s of 1949 were typically-durable members of their breed, and 562 was still hale and hearty when snapped on a Wakefield Road service three weeks after the trolleybuses had been replaced in April 1967. *Author*

Above:
Weymann bodied 48 chassis for both sections of the fleet in 1949-51, the 40 AEC Regent 9612E motorbuses being popular as the first eight-footers. No 29 entered service in January 1950, and gained its non-standard destination layout after a collision in 1956. It is seen climbing Morley Street in April 1967, soon after 2½ years temporary storage.   *Author*

Left:
The eight BUT 9611T trolleys were the last *new* vehicles for the system, having been sanctioned for an Undercliffe conversion which never materialised. Licensed in January 1951, 758 later had the first flashing trafficators fitted to a road vehicle in this country, and went for preservation in 1971.   *Author*

Above:
Bodywork detail distinguished the 7ft 6in-wide Weymann/BUTs of 1949 which had hailed from the Notts & Derby fleet in 1953 for a further 14-years duty. Alongside is a 1950 AEC of conventional appearance, whilst a Leeds Roe-bodied Regent or Daimler ticks over in the background. *L. W. Rowe*

Below:
To the author, the classic postwar Leeds bus is this style of Roe body on AEC Regent III chassis, purchased in quantity from 1949 to 1952. It represented the full-flowering of the prewar four-bay prototypes, and successive detail changes, right through to 1966 deliveries, only detracted from its appeal: No 497 was new in 1950, and gave 18 years sterling service. *Author*

Top left:

No 397 was one of 40 Leyland PD2/1s which also joined the fleet in 1950, and had perhaps the least-attractive version of Leyland's legendary highbridge body, with so much rubber glazing-strip in evidence. They were the mainstay of Bramley Depot's allocation throughout their lives, however, and lasted as long as their AEC counterparts. *C. Jones*

Centre left:

Just six Regent IIIs with Weymann bodies entered the fleet as a welcome foil to all the Roe products in 1952, and were some of the most pleasant looking vehicles to emerge from that source, immediately before depths were plumbed with the Orion design. Tailing 651 into the Central bus station is a 1948 Regent with the early-postwar style of Roe body.
L. W. Rowe

Below:

After a brief interlude of resuscitated prewar Regents, the Beeston and Lawnswood trams were effectively replaced in 1955/6 by 20 Metro-Cammell Orion-bodied Daimler CVG6s as well as the first AEC Regent Vs with exposed radiators. Introducing 'tin fronts' to the Leeds fleet, the Daimlers were an unexpected choice in being the first purchased since the postwar scramble for new buses. *Author*

Above:
By 1959, Leeds had at last resorted to 8ft-wide buses as standard policy. The Daimlers of that year were amongst the first 30-footers, causing a reversion to five-bay construction and, being fitted with well-styled Roe bodies, it was now the chassis front-end design which spoilt their appearance. No 505 is seen at Duncan Street/Vicar Lane junction.   *C. Jones*

Below:
The initial stages of trolleybus abandonment, coinciding with the need to replace early-postwar diesels, led to Bradford's acquisition of no less than 120 AEC Regent Vs between 1959 and 1965. Some were later painted in a reversed livery, but nothing could mask the utilitarian appearance of their Orion-style bodywork.   *C. Jones*

16
Hail, and Farewell!

The local bodybuilding firm of Charles H. Roe was so strongly identified with the region's bus fleets throughout its existence of almost 70 years, that it is appropriate to close with a small tribute and illustrate some notable designs in its production history.

Having been founded on the remains of the pioneer Railless Electric Traction Company, essential early diversification into goods vehicle and charabanc building was soon rendered unnecessary by steadily growing business with municipal bus operators, to the extent that coach bodywork never subsequently amounted to more than a fraction of Roe's output. Whilst small independents had always featured in its order books, there was a significant breakthrough into the major company fleets at the end of the 1920s. Throughout the following decade, it became particularly associated with centre-entrance double-deck bodywork, and also successful continuation of composite construction when rivals were becoming committed to metal-framed designs. A further hallmark at that time was a divergence of double-deck and saloon styling, through the establishment of separate design sections for the two types of vehicle.

Only a short interruption to bus work occurred after 1940, as Roe was one of the companies selected to produce utility bodywork, and a necessary recourse to timber framework was no handicap, given its more extensive development of that material in modern designs than had occurred with most other major bodybuilders. Acquisition by Park Royal in 1947 (which in turn was bought out by AEC two years later) brought little change to the initial reversion to prewar standards, and although there was some cross-fertilisation in styling, a distinctive appearance was maintained in most cases, until the cessation of front-engined chassis production. It was also gradually reasserted on the more amorphous outline of rear-engined 'deckers, culminating in the well-proportioned style developed out of a Leeds specification, for the West Yorkshire PTE's requirements in the late-1970s.

Earlier, acquisition of the Associated Commercial Vehicles empire (ie AEC group) by Leyland in 1962 had improved rather than diminished Roe's prospects, particularly after closure of Park Royal's works in July 1980. Selection as a bodybuilder for Leyland's Olympian double-deck chassis in 1981 seemed to augur well; the addition to the production lines of the new high-specification Doyen coach body, after a nine-year absence of single-deck output, promised even better. The mid-1984 announcement that closure was imminent was therefore a most unexpected development, and the last products were driven out of the plant on 31 August 1984.

Above:
By 1932, Leyland Titans had joined the West Riding fleet in quantity, but the tramway-replacement TD2s of that year were notable for their centre entrances. The 48-seat bodies were also the first Roe products bought new by the company; No 18 (HL 5323) gave 16 years valliant service. *Leyland Vehicles Ltd/Courtesy G. Lumb*

Below:
The 1949 design for Leeds was just about the ideal shape within the constraints then applying, and illustrates the form the London RT might have assumed with advantage; No 669 was a 1952 delivery on an AEC Regent III chassis. *Author*